RONALDO

MATT AND TOM OLDFIELD

ULTIMATE
FOOTBALL HEROES

RONALDO

FROM THE PLAYGROUND
TO THE PITCH

DINO

Published by Dino Books
an imprint of John Blake Publishing Ltd
3 Bramber Court, 2 Bramber Road,
London W14 9PB, England

www.johnblakepublishing.co.uk

www.facebook.com/johnblakebooks ▪
twitter.com/jblakebooks ▪

First published in paperback in 2017

ISBN: 978 1 78 606 405 9

British Library Cataloguing-in-Publication Data:

A catalogue record for this book is available from the British Library.

Design by www.envydesign.co.uk

Printed in Great Britain by CPI Group (UK) Ltd

1 3 5 7 9 10 8 6 4 2

Papers used by John Blake Publishing are natural, recyclable products made from
wood grown in sustainable forests. The manufacturing processes conform to the
environmental regulations of the country of origin.

Every attempt has been made to contact the relevant copyright-holders, but some
were unobtainable. We would be grateful if the appropriate people could contact us.

John Blake Publishing is an imprint of Bonnier Publishing
www.bonnierpublishing.co.uk

For Noah and Nico,
Southampton's future strikeforce.

ULTIMATE
FOOTBALL HEROES

Matt Oldfield is an accomplished writer and the editor-in-chief
of football review site Of Pitch & Page. Tom Oldfield is a freelance
sports writer and the author of biographies on Cristiano Ronaldo,
Arsène Wenger and Rafael Nadal.

Cover illustration by Dan Leydon.
To learn more about Dan visit danleydon.com
To purchase his artwork visit etsy.com/shop/footynews
Or just follow him on Twitter @danleydon

TABLE OF CONTENTS

ACKNOWLEDGEMENTS

First of all, I'd like to thank John Blake Publishing –
and particularly my editor James Hodgkinson – for
giving me the opportunity to work on these books
and for supporting me throughout. Writing stories for
the next generation of football fans is both an honour
and a pleasure.

I wouldn't be doing this if it wasn't for Tom. I owe
him so much and I'm very grateful for his belief in
me as an author. I feel like Robin setting out on a
solo career after a great partnership with Batman. I
hope I do him (Tom, not Batman) justice with these
new books.

Next up, I want to thank my friends for keeping

me sane during long hours in front of the laptop. Pang, Will, Mills, Doug, John, Charlie – the laughs and the cups of coffee are always appreciated.

I've already thanked my brother but I'm also very grateful to the rest of my family, especially Melissa, Noah and of course Mum and Dad. To my parents, I owe my biggest passions: football and books. They're a real inspiration for everything I do.

Finally, I couldn't have done this without Iona's encouragement and understanding during long, work-filled weekends. Much love to you.

CHAPTER 1

EUROPEAN GLORY

Cristiano had already won so many trophies during his amazing career – one Spanish league title, two Spanish cups, three Premier League titles, three English cups, three Champions League trophies and three Ballon d'Ors. But he still felt something was missing. That something was an international trophy with Portugal.

And on 10 July 2016, he was one step away from achieving that dream. With his confidence and goals, Cristiano had led his team all the way to the Euro 2016 final. At the Stade de France, Portugal faced a France team with home advantage and world-class players like Paul Pogba and Antoine Griezmann.

Portugal were the underdogs, but they had the best player in Europe – Cristiano – and he had never been more determined to win.

After their coach, Fernando Santos, had given his team talk in the dressing room, it was time for the senior players to speak. Nani went first and then it was Cristiano's turn.

'We've done so well to get this far,' their captain told them. 'One more win and we will go down in history. We will return home as heroes!'

The whole squad cheered. Together they could become the champions of Europe.

Cristiano stood with his eyes closed for the Portuguese national anthem. He didn't mumble the words; he shouted them at the top of his voice. He loved his country and he wanted to do them proud on the pitch.

After seven minutes, Cristiano got the ball just inside the French half. As he turned to attack, Dimitri Payet fouled him. The game carried on but Cristiano was still on the ground, holding his left knee and screaming in agony.

Oww!

As the physios used the magic spray and rubbed his knee with an ice pack, Cristiano winced. The injury didn't look good. He put his hands to his face to hide the tears.

Dimitri came over to say sorry for his tackle, but Cristiano was too upset to reply. Eventually, he stood up and limped off the field. On the touchline, he tested his leg – it didn't feel good but he wanted to keep playing.

'Are you sure?' João Mário said to him as he walked back onto the pitch.

'I have to try!' Cristiano told him.

But a minute later, he collapsed to the ground. On his big day, Cristiano was in too much pain to continue. He kept shaking his head – he couldn't believe his bad luck.

'You have to go off,' Nani told him, giving his friend a hug. 'We'll do our skipper proud, I promise!'

Cristiano wasn't ready to give up yet, though. The physios put a bandage around his knee and he went back on again. But when he tried to run, he had to stop. He signalled to the bench: 'I need to come off'.

He ripped off his captain's armband. 'Wear this,' Cristiano said to Nani, putting the armband on him. 'And win this final!'

'Yes, we'll win this for you!' Pepe shouted.

As he was carried off on a stretcher, Cristiano cried and cried. The most important match of his life was over.

It was 0–0 at half-time and Cristiano was there in the dressing room to support his teammates. 'Stick together and keep fighting hard!' he told them.

In the second-half, he was there on the bench, biting his fingernails and, in his head, kicking every ball. Every time Portugal nearly scored, he was up on his feet ready to celebrate. Just before striker Éder went on as a sub, Cristiano looked him in the eyes and said, 'Be strong. You're going to score the winner.'

But after ninety minutes, it was still 0–0. Cristiano walked around giving encouragement to the tired players. It was tough not being out on the pitch, but he could still play his part. After 109 minutes, Éder got the ball, shrugged off the French defender and sent a rocket of a shot into the bottom corner.

Goooooooooooooaaaaaaaaalllllllllllllllllllll!!!!!!!!!!!

Cristiano went wild, throwing his arms in the air and jumping up and down. The whole Portugal squad celebrated together. They were so close to victory now.

For the last ten minutes, Cristiano stood with Santos as a second manager. He hobbled along the touchline, shouting instructions to the players.

Run! Defend! Take your time!

At the final whistle, Cristiano let out a howl of happiness as the tears rolled down his cheeks again. He hugged each of his teammates and thanked them.

'No, thank *you!*' Éder said to him. 'Without you, I wouldn't have scored that goal!'

'I told you we'd do it!' Pepe laughed.

Cristiano took his shirt off and threw it into the crowd. They had to give him another one so that he could do his captain's duty – collecting the Euro 2016 trophy.

He climbed the steps slowly, giving high-fives to

the fans he passed. The trophy had red and green ribbons, the colours of Portugal's flag. As Cristiano lifted the trophy, the whole team cheered. He kissed it and then passed it on to the other players. No words could describe the joy that Cristiano was feeling.

It was at Manchester United and Real Madrid that he became a superstar, but Cristiano's incredible journey to the top of world football had begun at home in Portugal, with his family, on the island of Madeira. And so the Euro 2016 triumph was a way of saying thanks, for when life wasn't always easy growing up.

Without a difficult start in life, perhaps Cristiano wouldn't have had his amazing hunger to be the best, which turned a special gift into years of glory.

CHAPTER 2

DOLORES AND DINIS

'We're going to have another child?' Dolores asked the doctor when he told her the news. She was so shocked that she needed to hear it again. 'Are you sure? I can't believe it!'

Dolores and José Dinis Aveiro already had three children – daughters Elma and Katia, and son Hugo – and it had been eight years since Katia's birth. A fourth child was a real surprise.

'Yes, I'm certain,' the doctor confirmed. 'The news will bring great joy to your house, I'm sure!'

Dolores loved children, but she was worried. Life on the Portuguese island of Madeira was hard. The weather was always good, but many of the people were fed up. A lot of folk were unemployed, especially in the area of Funchal where they lived. The wealthy tourists stayed in the fancy seaside hotels and they never travelled far to spend their money.

Dolores worked hard making wicker baskets to sell, but Dinis had returned from the army and couldn't find a good job. Sometimes, they could only afford to eat bread and soup. And now, they would have another mouth to feed.

'Dinis, what are we going to do?' Dolores said when she got home. She was crying tears of both happiness and sadness.

Space was also a problem. The family lived in the house of Dinis's parents, but there would now be six of them. They didn't have any money to rent a house of their own.

'We'll just have to do the best we can,' Dinis replied.

Dolores agreed. Her fourth child would have a tough start in life but she would do everything possible to make sure they escaped the poverty of

Madeira. She was a very strong person and her son or daughter would be too.

When they found out it would be a boy, Dolores's sister suggested the name 'Cristiano' and they liked it. Dolores also chose to call her son after the actor and President of the United States of America, Ronald Reagan.

'It's a good name – the name of an honourable and successful person,' she told her family. Everyone agreed.

Cristiano Ronaldo dos Santos Aveiro.

Cristiano was a big, heavy baby. As the doctor placed him down in a bed, he laughed.

'It's a very good sign,' he said. 'Weighing that much, he could be a footballer!'

Both Dolores and Dinis loved that idea. Dolores was a Sporting Lisbon fan, and her favourite player was their star winger, Luís Figo. Dinis had played football as a young boy and often watched the local team, Andorinha. His friend Fernando Sousa, who would be Cristiano's godfather, was the captain of Andorinha. There were plenty of connections with football.

'Let's hope so!' Dinis replied with a smile.

It wouldn't be easy but anything was possible. They knew that very few youngsters had the special talent to become professional footballers, but it could be the perfect way for their son to leave the poverty of Funchal behind and make a new life somewhere else.

CHAPTER 3

STREET FOOTBALL IN FUNCHAL

'Katia, please make sure that Cristiano does his homework after school,' Dolores shouted as she left in the morning. 'Then – and only then – can he go out and play football!'

The local council had finally found a home for the family in Quinta do Falcão, one of the poorest areas of Funchal. The walls hadn't been painted and the roof often leaked, but there were three bedrooms: one for Dolores and Dinis, one for Elma and Katia, and one for Hugo and Cristiano.

'A proper home for our family!' Dolores said happily, when they had their first dinner together there.

However, in order to pay the rent, everyone was working harder than ever. Dolores had a new job in the kitchen of a hotel, Dinis was working at Andorinha, and Elma and Hugo had both left school early to earn money for the family. This meant that Katia, who was only fourteen, was in charge of her younger brother, Cristiano. He had an innocent smile like an angel but he could be very naughty.

'As soon as you finish your work, you can go out and play,' Katia reminded him as they walked home from school. 'I can help you but you've got to get it done first. OK?'

Cristiano nodded and when they got in, he took off his backpack and opened his books at the kitchen table. Katia went upstairs to change her clothes and when she came down, her brother had gone.

'Cristiano?' she called out. She thought he might have gone to the toilet, but the bathroom was empty. She went out into the street.

'Cristiano! Cristiano!'

But it was no use; the little rascal had escaped through the back door to go and play football.

'Just wait until Mum finds out!' Katia said to herself.

There weren't many parks in Quinta do Falcão, or big open spaces. If Cristiano didn't want to walk miles to the nearest beach, the only place to play football was in the street. The conditions were far from perfect. The roads were uneven, with obstacles everywhere, and they weren't very flat either. They used rocks as goalposts and blocked the road for as long as they could.

'There's a car coming!' someone would shout eventually, and the whole match stopped.

The rocks were moved, but once the car had gone past, the rocks returned and the match restarted. This went on and on until darkness and dinner. If they couldn't find a real football, they played with a plastic bottle or a ball of paper. Nothing could stop them.

In fact, the only good thing about Cristiano's first 'pitch' was that he had to learn brilliant close control and the art of dribbling in small spaces. He was, of course, a natural. His feet were a blur as he ran forward with the ball glued to his foot. Cristiano would dance with the ball, doing stepovers and flicks to beat the defenders. He watched the older kids playing in the street and learned all of their tricks. It never took him long.

Sometimes, there would be a crowd of locals watching and Cristiano loved to entertain them.

Wow! Olé!

He could kick the ball well with both feet, so opponents never knew if he would go right or left. The one-on-one battle was his favourite and when he was at his best, no one could tackle him. He quickly made a name for himself.

'Cristiano, you're on my team!'

'We've got more players, but you've got Cristiano!'

He loved football but he absolutely hated losing. Even at the age of six, defeat wasn't an option for him. Cristiano was the most competitive kid in Quinta do Falcão, and that was one of the reasons why he always won.

'That was definitely a goal!' he shouted, with his

arms up in the air. Cristiano had dribbled past three defenders and shot past the goalkeeper. But without goalposts or a referee, there were sometimes big arguments.

'No, that would have gone over the crossbar!' Vitor, one of the other boys, said, shaking his head.

His teammates accepted the decision, but Cristiano wanted his wonder goal. 'No way – my shot was way below head height!' he screamed, kicking at the dirt. He didn't give up easily; football was all about winning and being the best.

If no one was around to play with him, Cristiano would find a wall nearby and practise his shooting for hours and hours. He was obsessed with improving every aspect of his game, but it was the battles on the pitch that he loved most. Victory was the best feeling in the world and he was determined to feel it every day.

As soon as the match was over, Cristiano became his normal, funny self again, but while he was out on his 'pitch', he was totally focused and totally serious.

'See you same time tomorrow!' he shouted as they

all left to go home. Already, he couldn't wait for the next day.

Cristiano tried to creep back into his house but Dolores was waiting for him, and she wasn't happy.

'What did I tell you?' she said, grabbing him by the ear. 'I told you that you could play football once your homework was finished. Is it finished?'

Cristiano looked at the floor and shook his head.

'And have you swept the floors like I asked you to? It doesn't look like it!' she shouted, moving a bit of dirt with her shoe.

'I'm sorry!' Cristiano said and burst into tears.

His punishment was over. 'Son, I know you love football and I don't want to ever stop you from following your dream,' Dolores said, stroking his hair. 'But you must also tell the truth and help your family.'

'You're way too good to be playing with those guys,' he told Cristiano. 'I'm playing at Andorinha now – you should come to training with me!'

Cristiano liked that idea. His dad was the club's caretaker, his godfather was the captain, and his brother Hugo was playing for the club, too. It made a lot of sense. He often went along to watch anyway, so why not go and play?

'Nuno's right,' Dinis said when his son told him about the plan. 'It's time for you to start playing proper football.'

Proper football was more different than Cristiano had expected. The Andorinha pitch was completely flat and everyone had their own team shirt. They warmed up with lots of running and stretches. And the training sessions weren't just a big match: the coach put out cones and made them do passing and dribbling exercises.

'It's like being a professional!' Cristiano told Nuno happily. He had developed his style and confidence in street football, but at a football club he could learn about tactics and how to make the most of his talent.

Cristiano was training with boys who were two or three years older than him, and they looked much bigger and stronger. Cristiano was tall for an eight-year-old but he was still very skinny. When you performed as many tricks as he did, defenders were always going to foul you. At first, the physical battle was pretty scary. In the match at the end of training, one of the boys slid in for a crunching tackle and Cristiano went flying through the air.

Oww!

He got back to his feet and limped away.

'Are you OK?' the coach asked.

'Yes, I'm fine,' Cristiano replied. 'Don't worry, I can look after myself!'

He didn't want to show any weakness in front of his new teammates. He wasn't going to let a bit of pain stop him.

It took a few sessions for his competitive edge to kick in, but Cristiano was soon the best player in the team. He was as quick with the ball at his feet as he was without it, and he dazzled defenders with his magical dribbling. His shooting got better and better and he scored lots of goals in the seven-a-side and eleven-a-side matches they played every week.

'Well played, Cry-Baby!' Ricardo, his teammate, said with a smile after yet another victory. 'I didn't see a single tear today.'

Cristiano didn't like his new nickname but he knew that it was just a friendly joke. He was very passionate about football and winning, and he couldn't help showing his emotions.

If a teammate was selfish and tried to score himself, rather than passing to Cristiano, he cried.

'I was right there – I would have scored!'

If a teammate dared to criticise him for not passing, he cried.

'I'm the best player and I'm helping us to win!'

And if the team lost a match, he cried and cried.

'I can't believe it – that was the referee's fault!'

As long as Cristiano kept playing so well, his teammates didn't mind. In one game, Andorinha were losing 2–0 at half-time. Cristiano had missed a few chances and so he came into the dressing room with tears of frustration rolling down his cheeks. He sat on his own in the corner with his back to the other players. After a minute, Ricardo went over to him.

'Calm down! There's still plenty of time for you to win the game for us.'

Cristiano nodded and took a deep breath. In the second-half, he turned his anger into gold. By the final whistle, they had won 3–2 and he was the hero.

'You love a bit of drama, don't you?' Ricardo laughed as they celebrated.

As soon as the game was over, Ronaldo always went back to being a normal, funny boy. 'Yes, but what would you guys do without me?' he replied.

CHAPTER 5

C.D. NACIONAL

After retiring from football, Fernando Sousa became a
youth team coach at C.D. Nacional, one of the biggest
clubs in Madeira. As well as training his players, he
also spent time looking for new talent on the island.

'Have you seen that new winger at Andorinha?'
one of the scouts asked him. 'He's incredible!'

'I keep hearing about this kid!' Fernando replied.
Word always spread very quickly about 'the next big
thing'. 'I'll have to go down and see him for myself.'

When he arrived at Andorinha and the match
kicked off, he couldn't believe it – the 'new winger'
that everyone was talking about was his godson,
Cristiano!

'Wow, when did he become so good?' Fernando said to himself.

With each goal that Andorinha scored, Fernando's smile got bigger and bigger. Fernando hadn't seen Cristiano for a few years and he was now a completely different player. In fact, he was the best young player that Fernando had ever seen. At ten years old, he was miles ahead of any other kid on the pitch.

'I have to sign him for Nacional!' Fernando decided after only a few minutes.

It would be a very difficult task, however, even though he knew the family well. Cristiano was a fan of their rivals, C.S. Marítimo. The club had a close relationship with Andorinha and many young players progressed from one team to the other. The Marítimo stadium was also much closer to Cristiano's home.

'They have a great record of developing young players and they just got to the Portuguese cup final,' Dinis explained when Fernando went to speak to him about Cristiano's future.

'I understand, but Nacional will still make an offer and we'll see what happens.'

Bernardino Rosa was the Marítimo scout who wanted to sign Cristiano. He kept telling everyone at the club about the amazing young winger that he had found.

'He's got so much potential but we've got to move fast!'

Some of the coaches at Marítimo weren't so sure about signing Cristiano, however, and the contract talks slowed down.

'It's odd but I think they might be losing interest,' Dinis admitted to Fernando.

'We want Cristiano to go where he's really wanted and valued,' Dolores added. 'At the moment, that doesn't look like Marítimo.'

That gave Nacional plenty of hope. When Bernardino missed a key meeting with Andorinha, the club chose to accept Nacional's offer instead: two sets of kits and twenty footballs for Cristiano.

'What a bargain!' Fernando said. He was delighted with his big new signing.

'You're going to love it here,' he said as he showed the family around the brand new Nacional youth academy facilities.

Cristiano looked like someone had shown him the world's biggest sweet shop. 'This place is incredible!' he said to his dad. He could already tell that the level was higher here.

'This is your first step towards the big time, son,' Dinis told him, suddenly looking very serious. 'If you listen to the coaches and learn from them, this could be the start of something amazing.'

Cristiano nodded. He was desperate to make his professional football dream come true. Even at the age of ten, Cristiano was fully focused on becoming the best in the world. If Dolores asked about his education, his answer was always the same: football was his priority, not school. Eventually, she let her son make his own decision.

'If this is what you really want, then do it and I won't stand in your way,' she said, hoping that she was doing the right thing.

Pedro Talhinhas was one of the Nacional youth coaches. He had heard about Cristiano's reputation but this was to be the first time he had seen him in action. He was very excited.

'Welcome!' he said, shaking the youngster's hand. 'I hope you're ready to work hard!'

In the training drills, Cristiano showed that he had good ball control, lots of skill and good power with both feet. He had passed the first test, but what about the match at the end? Pedro would be looking for different talents there.

It was only Cristiano's first session at the club, but he still couldn't tame his determination to win. It brought out the best but also the worst in him. Cristiano dribbled towards goal on his own, completely ignoring his new teammates, who called for him to pass. He did some nice tricks and stepovers but then he got tackled and lost the ball. The other players weren't happy.

'Why didn't you pass?' they asked.

In the heat of battle, Cristiano was making

enemies, rather than friends. 'Because I'm better than all of you!' he replied angrily.

Pedro was disappointed by the youngster's arrogance, but he had seen it many times before. In order to be a great street footballer, you had to show that kind of self-confidence. However, in order to be a great club footballer, you had to be smarter and a lot less selfish.

Once the training session was over, Pedro sat down with Cristiano and told him: 'You have a very special talent but unless you learn to play with others, you won't succeed. This type of football is about teamwork and your new teammates are excellent. You have to trust them in order to win.'

Cristiano listened carefully to his coach, as his dad had told him to do. In the next session, he passed to his teammates more often, but he still struggled to be nice to them.

'I'm in space – pass it!' Cristiano shouted all game long.

If the pass didn't arrive, he threw his arms up in

the air. He still cried a lot. 'Come on, you've got to do better than that!'

After a few weeks, Pedro was happy with Cristiano's progress but there was one thing that still worried him. He decided to speak to Dolores.

'Does your son have a good appetite?' he asked.

'He's a young boy – he eats anything I put in front of him!' his mum replied, laughing.

'Does he eat much meat?'

'I'm afraid it depends on money. If I can afford to buy meat, I buy it. But some weeks, we just eat soup and bread.'

Pedro knew that Cristiano didn't come from a very wealthy family, and a good balanced diet could be very expensive.

'I understand that it's very difficult, but please do your best to give him more meat and fish. He's a great player but he's very skinny. We need to toughen him up before the defenders snap him in half like a twig!'

CHAPTER 6

SCOUTED BY SPORTING

Aurélio Pereira was a very important man in Portuguese football. At top club Sporting Lisbon, he had signed some of the nation's best recent footballers: Paulo Futre, Simão Sabrosa and, best of all, Luis Figo. He knew top talent when he saw it, and he was about to see a kid from Madeira.

Cristiano was getting better and better at Nacional. He was the star player, helping them win the regional Under-13 championship. His magical skills lit up the local leagues and grabbed the attention of bigger clubs across the country, too. By the time Cristiano was twelve, Fernando and Dinis were discussing the next move for their golden boy.

'He's too good to stay on this island,' Fernando argued. 'If he stays here, he will waste his special gift.'

Dinis agreed and so Fernando got in touch with his friend João Marques de Freitas, who knew lots of people at Sporting Lisbon.

'OK, let me see what I can do,' João replied. The first person he called was Aurélio Pereira.

'A friend of mine says that his godson is the real deal,' he said. 'I know you must hear that all the time, but I trust his opinion. The kid lives in Madeira. What should I do?'

Aurélio decided to trust João and his friend. 'OK, I'll send a scout to watch him.'

The scout arrived at a tournament that Nacional were playing in, but Cristiano wasn't in the team. Instead, he was on the sideline, doing keepy-uppies and flicks. The ball never touched the ground, even when Cristiano tried his most difficult tricks. His feet were a blur.

The scout was very impressed. 'It was like watching a magic show!' he reported to Aurélio. 'I've never seen anyone with so many skills.'

Aurélio called João back straight away. 'Tell this kid to come over for a trial.'

Cristiano had never even left Madeira before. Fernando took him to the airport, but after that, he was travelling on his own. He was quite used to that. At Nacional, his dad came to watch his matches but Cristiano always went to training alone. He could look after himself but flying to Lisbon was something very different. Cristiano had never been so nervous.

When the plane landed, Aurélio was there to meet him. On the football pitch, he was loud and aggressive, but in a new place with a new person, Cristiano was as quiet as a mouse. As they drove to the training ground, he stared out of the window. He had never seen so many cars and so many people. Lisbon was nothing like Madeira.

'It's a big city,' Aurélio said to break the silence. 'But it's a friendly city, I promise.'

As soon as Cristiano saw the football pitches in the distance, he calmed down and his confidence returned. 'This is what I'm here for and I'm ready to

shine,' he thought to himself. He wasn't afraid
of anything.

When they arrived, Aurélio gave him a Sporting kit
and introduced him to Paulo Cardoso, a youth coach.
Cristiano got changed, did some stretches, and then
ran onto the field. One of the other kids passed the
ball to him and so focused was Cristiano on what he
was going to do next, that he let the ball roll under
his foot.

He was very annoyed at himself, but he would
have plenty more chances. The next time he got the
ball, he pulled off an awesome bit of skill. Before the
defender even knew what was going on, Cristiano
was flying past him down the wing.

'Wow!' Paulo muttered. 'That's special.'

Cristiano showed off his full bag of tricks. He
scored goals with his right foot and goals with his left
foot. It was an absolute masterclass and older kids
came over from other pitches to watch.

At the end of the first day, Paulo wrote a report
for Aurélio. It was full of praise, and so on day two
Aurélio went down to watch. It was hard to believe

that this kid was the same shy lad that had sat in silence in his car two days earlier. Cristiano was already telling his teammates what to do and where to pass the ball. Quite a few of them were older than him but they seemed to accept his leadership.

'He's certainly a brave character!' Aurélio laughed to himself.

It didn't take long for Aurélio to make a judgement – Cristiano was exactly what Sporting Lisbon needed. The youngster still had a few days left in his trial, but they had already started to prepare contracts.

'His natural ability is incredible and we can teach him the rest,' Aurélio told the club's owners. 'He could be the future of this team.'

The next step was a trip to Madeira to Cristiano's parents. In a hotel, Aurélio explained Sporting's offer: 'In Lisbon, we would look after Cristiano well. He would live with the other boys in our youth centre, as part of the Sporting family. He would still go to school every day and he wouldn't be allowed to play football unless he behaved well.'

'Good luck with that!' Dolores thought.

'We would pay for you to fly over and visit him three times a year and there will be a yearly wage of 10,000 euros.'

The money would be very useful for the family, but Dolores was worried about letting her son leave. He was still only twelve years old. He would have to grow up very quickly in a big, new city and his mother wouldn't be there to protect him.

'Thank you, we'll need to think about it,' she told Aurélio.

'Mum, I want to go!' Cristiano begged. This was the chance of a lifetime. The only thing he had ever wanted to do was become a professional footballer.

'No problem, take your time and talk about,' Aurélio said. He didn't want to put any pressure on the family.

In the end, Dolores accepted that it was the right move for her son. By going to Lisbon, he was escaping a life of poverty in Madeira. She wouldn't have to worry about him drinking alcohol and getting involved in crime. Football would keep him on a good path.

As they said their goodbyes at the airport, everyone was crying.

'Good luck, my darling, we'll miss you!' Dolores said, kissing him on the cheeks. 'Be a good boy and write us letters every week. Fight for your dream!'

'I'll be looking out for you on TV!' Hugo joked.

It was a sad day, but Cristiano had a very bright future ahead of him.

CHAPTER 7

LIFE IN LISBON: OFF THE PITCH

'How is life in Lisbon?' Dolores asked on the phone. Her youngest son had been away from home for a month now and she missed him a lot. She wanted to know what exciting things he had been doing in Portugal's capital city.

Cristiano took a deep breath, but he couldn't help crying. 'Mum, I want to come home,' he said.

Back in Madeira, he had always loved his freedom. But freedom in Lisbon was scary. In Madeira, he walked everywhere and he knew every place and every person. Life was relaxed and friendly. But in Lisbon, he didn't know anyone and he had to take buses and underground trains on his own. At first, it was really difficult.

'Excuse me, how do I get to Telheiras?' he asked again and again, but everyone was too busy to help him. Alone in a new city, Cristiano took the wrong train and got lost. Everything was so big and confusing. In the end, he arrived late for his first day at his new school. The teacher was calling the register as he entered the classroom.

'Cristiano Ronaldo?'

He put his hand up. 'Yes, I'm here.'

As soon as he spoke, his classmates started laughing at him. Cristiano didn't understand what was so funny, but everyone was looking at him. Did he look like an alien? Had he forgotten to wear trousers? He hated being the new kid and he could feel himself getting hot and angry.

'Don't be so rude!' the teacher shouted at her class. 'Cristiano has come all the way from Madeira – please be nice and welcome him.'

He had never thought about his accent before, but clearly he spoke in a different way from the others.

Cristiano could hear the boys mocking him. As he looked around, he also saw that he dressed in a different way from the others. He was wearing an old T-shirt that his cousin had passed on to him, whereas his classmates wore new clothes from the coolest brands. He didn't fit in at all.

Life wasn't much better at the Sporting youth centre, either. Cristiano was two years younger than all of the other boys. They played in a different team and wanted to hang out with their teammates, not a little twelve-year-old. In the evenings once football training was over, Cristiano sat in his room, thinking about home.

'Don't give up, my darling,' Dolores said once he had explained everything to her. It was awful to hear her son sound so upset when she was so many miles away. She wished she could at least give him a big hug. 'You'll make friends and then it will all be better. Soon, you'll forget all about us in Madeira!'

'Never!' Cristiano replied straight away. He looked at his phone card – he was nearly out of time already.

Fortunately, Aurélio was around to keep an eye on him and one of the Sporting Lisbon youth coaches also took Cristiano under his wing. Leonel Pontes was from Madeira too and he knew exactly how hard it was to adapt to life in the big city.

'The first few months are the worst, I promise,' he told Cristiano when he invited him to his house for dinner. 'I can remember crying into my pillow every night.'

Leonel could see that the boy was holding back the tears. 'It's OK to be homesick, you know? It's good to talk about your emotions, rather than keep them bottled up inside. It's not a sign of weakness.'

Cristiano nodded. He was very grateful for Leonel's support, especially when his own family was so far away. He still missed home a lot but he was determined to achieve his football dream, no matter what.

'I'm here to make history,' Cristiano told himself whenever he felt sad.

It took time, but eventually Lisbon felt like home

and he felt happy there. By the age of fourteen, he had made new friends, but he was more focused on football than ever.

One time, in the middle of the night, Hugo Pina woke up to find his roommate awake and fully dressed. 'Cristiano, where are you going?' he whispered.

'I'm going to the gym,' Cristiano replied. 'Do you want to come?'

Hugo shook his head and closed his eyes again. 'No, you're crazy – I want to sleep!'

Cristiano was always looking for ways to improve. He would train with his teammates during the day and then do his own personal training at night. He worked harder than everyone else. He was never satisfied, even when it came to things he was really good at, like ball control, dribbling and sprinting.

But there was one thing that Cristiano was really desperate to improve – his strength. He was still very skinny and if he was going to compete against big defenders, he needed to toughen up.

'I've got the skill to beat them, but what's the point if I'm too weak to get the ball in the first place?' he told Hugo.

He started by doing sit-ups and press-ups in his bedroom. Then he tied weights around his ankles and went out running. He waited for the traffic lights to go green and then he raced cars up the steep hill.

'What is he doing?!' the drivers thought as they saw a young boy running alongside them.

But Cristiano still didn't feel that his muscles were growing quickly enough. So when he saw older, more powerful players lifting weights in the gym, he decided to copy them.

'You're only fourteen!' Hugo told him. If he wasn't careful, Cristiano could injure himself. 'Those guys are huge – there's no way that you should lift weights that heavy.'

But once Cristiano had made up his mind, there was no stopping him. Cristiano had heard some of the older players talking about how a squad player had hurt himself badly after lifting with poor form, and Cristiano knew he couldn't risk his own health by making the same mistakes. After all, you couldn't play football with a bad back. So, after a few sessions with a coach to learn exactly how to lift weights safely, he spent hours at the gym every night until the club put a lock on the door. Even that didn't stop him, though. It was a challenge and he worked until he achieved it

'It just means that I have less time to reach my targets,' he said to Hugo. 'I'm going to start eating dinner later, once I've been to the gym. And if I have to, I'll just climb in through the window!'

CHAPTER 8

LIFE IN LISBON: ON THE PITCH

'I'll take this,' Cristiano shouted when his team won a corner in training. Even when Lisbon life off the pitch was difficult, he felt completely at home *on* the football pitch. It was where he belonged.

The other Under-15s players were too shocked to argue. Cristiano had been moved up to the higher age group and so he was a year younger than all of them. But instead of being humble, he was taking charge. Who did he think he was?

'I'll take this,' Cristiano shouted when his team won a free kick.

They were prepared for his arrogance this time. 'Wait a minute, this is your first—'

But before they could complete the sentence, the referee blew the whistle and Cristiano hit a powerful, swerving shot into the bottom corner of the net.

Goooooooooooooooooooooooooooooaaaaaaaaaaaaa aaaaaaaaaaaaalllllllllllllllllllllllllllllllllllllllll!!!!!!!!!!

He celebrated by winking at his teammates. He had plenty of confidence.

'I'll take this,' Cristiano shouted when his team won a penalty.

This time, no one complained. It didn't take his teammates long to work out that it was easier not to argue with him. He was the best player they had ever played with. As long as they played to Cristiano's rules, they always won. But if they tried to take too many shots or didn't pass to him when he called for the ball, he went wild.

'What are you doing?' he shouted, kicking the grass in frustration.

If the team was winning 5–0, most of the players started to relax, but not Cristiano.

'Come on, let's keep attacking!' he screamed at the defenders. He always wanted more.

He didn't wear the captain's armband, but he quickly became the leader. Cristiano told them what to do and they listened. Hugo had never seen anyone who was so competitive and passionate. Failure just wasn't an option for him and that rubbed off on his teammates.

But there were also problems with Cristiano's attitude. He was still a very bad loser and he often got sent off for his tantrums. The coaches found it difficult to control him and give him advice.

'You've got to pass the ball earlier!' Leonel shouted when Cristiano lost the ball, but he knew his young player wouldn't listen. Instead, he did exactly the same thing again but this time he didn't get tackled and scored an incredible goal. That was just Cristiano's style.

And the other problem was his teammates. Some liked playing with Cristiano but there were others who didn't like his aggressive style. Ricardo Quaresma played on the left side of the front three, with Cristiano on the right. They were the two stars of the team, but they were rivals as much as teammates.

For Hugo in central midfield, life was very difficult.

If he passed to the right to Cristiano, Ricardo complained, and if he passed to the left to Ricardo, Cristiano complained.

'I can't win!' Hugo moaned, but they did always win, even if Cristiano and Ricardo never passed to each other.

'It's working at the moment but it could all end in trouble,' Leonel said in a discussion with Aurélio. 'At some point, Cristiano will have to learn to play *with* other very talented players.'

Normally, Sporting Lisbon coaches liked to let their youngsters learn from their own mistakes, but sometimes they had to teach lessons themselves.

There was one fixture that Cristiano had been looking forward to all season long: Marítimo away, the chance to return to Madeira and see his family and friends.

'I can't wait to come home!' he told Dolores as the game drew near.

'We can't wait either!' she replied. The whole family was so excited about seeing their young superstar back on the island.

But in the week before the game, Cristiano's performances in training were terrible. He didn't pass to anyone and he kept fighting with his teammates. He was doing badly at school too. It just wasn't acceptable and so the coaches made a difficult decision.

'What do you mean I'm not going?!' Cristiano exploded. He was looking at the squad list for the Marítimo match and his name wasn't there. He checked again and again but it definitely wasn't there. Maybe it was a mistake? He couldn't believe it.

'I'm sorry but we expect our players to behave well in training,' Aurélio told him. He knew how much it would hurt Cristiano to miss the trip but they had to treat him like any other player. Just because he was their best player, didn't mean that he could do anything and get away with it. He had to learn that. He had broken the rules – it was as simple as that.

Cristiano stormed out of the room with tears streaming down his face. How could they do this to him? It was so unfair. He called his mum because he knew that she would support him.

'They won't let me come to Madeira!' he wailed.

'Why, what's happened?' Dolores asked. She had waited so long to see her son and now she would have to wait even longer. It was heart-breaking news.

Cristiano only told her half of the story and so when the Sporting Lisbon team arrived on the island for the big game, she was there to defend her son.

'How can you stop Cristiano from coming home?' she asked the coaches with anger written all over her face.

But when Aurélio explained the full situation to her, Dolores soon calmed down. She knew all about her son's hot temper on the football field and she understood that the punishment was necessary.

'I know that you're always so determined to win but you can't do it on your own,' she told him on the phone. 'You have to support your teammates, you have to share the ball, and you have to listen to your coaches. You'll only become the best if you do all of that.'

Cristiano was learning his lesson. It was time to grow up and fulfil his dream of becoming the world's best footballer.

CHAPTER 9

GETTING CLOSER

By the age of sixteen, Cristiano knew that he was getting closer and closer to the Sporting Lisbon first team. He was playing well for the Under-16s, the Under-17s, the Under-18s and the Reserves. He still had tantrums from time to time but his behaviour was much better than before. Surely it was only a matter of time before the coach, László Bölöni, called him up to the senior squad?

'Ricardo will make his debut soon,' Cristiano told his mum, who had moved to Lisbon to live with him. 'They haven't even asked me to train with the team yet. Why not?'

'Ricardo is two years older than you, that's why!'

Dolores replied, rolling her eyes. Her son was always so competitive. 'Try to be patient.'

That wasn't easy at all for someone like Cristiano. But one day, when he returned to the training ground after school, the Reserves coach called him into his office.

'The day has come!' he said with a big smile on his face. 'You'll be training with the first team this afternoon.'

'Yes!' Cristiano shouted, pumping his fist. He finally had the chance to show Bölöni that he was ready for the big time.

'Don't be too much of a show-off on your first day,' Dolores warned him when he called to tell her the news. But she knew that her son wouldn't listen.

When he entered the changing room, Cristiano suddenly got very nervous. He was really excited but what if it all went wrong? He sat quietly in the corner as the famous players like Mário Jardel and João Vieira Pinto arrived and got ready. He was next to his heroes but he didn't say a word. So many thoughts were going through his head:

Will this be my only chance to impress?

What can I do to make sure that they don't forget me?

With his heart beating faster than ever, Cristiano ran out onto the training field. But with so much pressure on himself, he couldn't relax and play his best football. He didn't do much wrong but he also didn't do anything amazing.

'How was it?' Dolores asked when he got home.

'I don't think I did enough,' Cristiano replied, sitting down on the sofa with a loud sigh. 'I couldn't show Bölöni just how good I can be.'

Cristiano trained with the first team for weeks but he wasn't getting any better. He was running out of time to catch Bölöni's eye.

'I watched you the other day,' Aurélio told him. 'You're not playing your natural game! Where has your passion and confidence gone? You need to become fearless again.'

Cristiano knew that his mentor was right. In order to become the best player in the world, he had to believe in himself. When he returned to training, he was a different player. The old Cristiano was back. He wanted the ball all the time and when he got it, he dared to do his trademark stepovers and nutmegs. If a trick didn't work, he did it again and again until it did work.

'Who do you think you are, kid?' one of the senior defenders asked angrily when Cristiano fouled him. Usually, the youngsters were too scared to tackle hard. The stars didn't like it when a teenager made a fool of them.

'I'm going to be the best player in the world,' he replied. There wasn't a smile on his face; it wasn't a joke. He was deadly serious.

Bölöni was pleased with Cristiano's progress. He still had more to learn about teamwork and tactics but he also worked hard in the gym every day to get stronger.

'He's more professional at the age of sixteen than most of our senior players are at the age of thirty!' Bölöni told his coaches.

Jardel would leave the club soon and Sporting would need a new attacker.

'Trust me – Cristiano is the future,' Bölöni went on. 'Next season, he'll be ready to shine.'

CHAPTER 10

BREAKTHROUGH

'He'll be better than Eusébio and Figo,' Bölöni
predicted at a press conference ahead of the 2002–
03 season.

The Portuguese journalists laughed. They had
heard good things about Cristiano but would he
really be better than the country's two greatest
ever players? It seemed very unlikely. And besides,
he was still only seventeen years old. Anything
could happen.

But Cristiano didn't mind the pressure, and
he loved the praise. He had an agent now, called
Jorge Mendes, who really believed in him. With
his support, Cristiano was ready to live up to

the expectations. In a pre-season friendly against Spanish team Real Betis, he came on for the final fifteen minutes.

'I need to make an impact,' Cristiano told himself as he ran onto the pitch wearing a Sporting Number 28 shirt that was far too big for him. He felt unstoppable.

When a Betis defender took a bad first touch, Cristiano used his pace to pounce. Then he used his skill to flick the ball away from the defender. As he ran towards goal, the goalkeeper came out, but Cristiano dribbled round him with ease. He was wide on the left side of the penalty area; the angle wasn't good for shooting with his left foot. So he slowed down, shifted the ball onto his right foot and curled the ball high over the defender's head and into the top corner of the net.

Goooooooooooooooooooooooooooooooaaaaaaaaaaaa aaaaaaaaaaaaaaaalllllllllllllllllllllllllllllll!!!!!!!!!!!!!!!

What a way to score his first Sporting goal! With the adrenaline pumping through his body, Cristiano felt like he could fly. It was the best feeling ever. He waved to his mum in the crowd and blew her a kiss.

'That's just the start!' he told his teammates as they hugged him.

It wasn't long before Cristiano was doing the same thing in the Portuguese Primeira Liga. Against Moreirense, he received the ball just inside the opposition half. Cristiano did what he did best; he ran past defenders and towards the goal. On the edge of the penalty area, he did a stepover to beat the last defender and as the goalkeeper rushed out, he lifted the ball over him.

Goooooooooooooooooooooooooooooooooooaaaaaaa aaaaaaaaaaallllllllllllllllllllllllllllllllll!!!!!!!!!!!!!!!!!!!

In the excitement, Cristiano took off his shirt and threw it into the crowd. The Sporting fans were going wild; they had a new hero. As he looked up into the stands and heard the supporters chanting his name, he knew that his dream was coming true. He was on the road to becoming a world-beater.

Before the final whistle, Cristiano added a second with a header from a corner. It was a match that he would never forget.

'Congratulations, the whole of Europe is watching

you now!' his new agent, Jorge Mendes, told him after the game. 'Inter Milan, Real Madrid, Manchester United – you could play for any club that you want.'

Cristiano couldn't believe that such massive teams wanted to sign him already. He always believed that he had a special talent but he'd thought it would take a few seasons to make a name for himself. Instead, it had taken a few months.

'Cool! When do I sign?' he asked Jorge.

'We'll wait until the summer and see what offers we get,' his agent replied.

Cristiano was very grateful for all of Sporting's support and coaching but the Primeira Liga wasn't one of the top leagues in the world. All of the best players played in Italy, Spain or England. So that was where he wanted to go.

Cristiano didn't start every game for Sporting but whenever he was on the pitch, the fans got excited. He was a born entertainer with the magical skills to win matches. Against Boavista, it was 1–1 with ten minutes to go. It was time for Cristiano.

He started out on the left wing but he wanted more of the ball. So as Sporting attacked, he made a great run towards the penalty area. When the pass came, he was one-on-one with the goalkeeper. Some youngsters might have panicked and hit the shot as hard as they could, but not Cristiano. He slowed down and calmly placed the ball into the bottom corner.

Goooooooooooooooooooooooooooooooooooooaaaaaaa aaaaaaaaaaalllllllllllllllllllllllllllllllllllll!!!!!!!!!!!!!!!!!!!!

Again, Cristiano took off his shirt as he celebrated with the supporters. He was the super-sub, the matchwinner.

'I will never get tired of scoring goals,' he told his mum. 'And winning, of course!'

By the end of the season, Cristiano had played in thirty matches for Sporting. He wasn't yet a consistent player but he was still only a teenager. Everyone could see his quality and potential. They spoke to Arsenal, Juventus, Valencia, Liverpool and Barcelona, but Jorge wasn't in a hurry.

'We have to wait for the right offer,' he said. 'At

your age, you don't want to go to a big club where you earn lots of money but just sit on the bench. You need to be playing football!'

Cristiano and Dolores nodded.

'Where would you like to play?' the agent asked.

'Spain or England,' Cristiano replied immediately. 'They're the best leagues.'

'Good, well let's wait until after the Toulon tournament.'

Cristiano was part of the Under-20 Portugal team that travelled to France. After a disappointing time at the Under-17 European Championships in Denmark, he was determined to do better in his second international competition.

'We've got a good team,' Cristiano told his teammates. Again, he had made himself the leader and no one argued. 'Get the ball to me and we'll win!'

Their first opponents were England. Cristiano knew that Arsenal, Manchester United and Liverpool would all be watching him closely. He couldn't wait to put on a show for them.

'This one's for Arsène Wenger!' he joked before kick-off.

From the first minute of the match, he terrorised the England defence. They were dazzled by his quick feet and bursts of pace. They couldn't get the ball off him at all. The only thing they could do was foul him. He ended his masterclass by scoring his team's third goal.

'Wow, you've got a lot to live up to now!' Jorge laughed. Cristiano's price tag was getting higher and higher.

Portugal finished top of their group and then beat Italy 3–1 in the final. Argentina's Javier Mascherano won Player of the Tournament but Cristiano was very close behind him.

The next day, the media printed a photo of the winning team. In the photo, one player was standing at the front with no shirt on and his arms up in the air. Yes, it was Cristiano – he was already acting like a superstar.

CHAPTER 11

MANCHESTER UNITED

Carlos Queiroz was then the assistant manager at Manchester United, but many years earlier, he had been the manager of Sporting Lisbon. Signing new players wasn't his job but he still kept a close eye on Portuguese football. When he first watched Cristiano play, he told Sir Alex Ferguson straight away.

'There's a young winger who is lighting up the Primeira Liga at the moment. You have to see him – he's incredible. They say he's going to be even better than Figo!'

Ferguson sent one of his scouts to watch Cristiano play and he said exactly the same thing: 'You need to sign this kid, and quickly, before another club gets him!'

United offered to buy Cristiano and then loan him back to Sporting for one more year but the club wanted to keep their young superstar for as long as possible.

'We won't give up yet,' Ferguson promised Carlos.

By August 2003, David Beckham had signed for Real Madrid and United now had a big gap to fill. At first, Ferguson wanted the Brazilian star Ronaldinho, but Barcelona won the race to sign him. United needed a young, skilful attacker and Carlos believed that Cristiano would be perfect.

Sporting were opening their new stadium and they asked if Manchester United would come and play a friendly against them. The team was tired after a long tour in the USA, but Ferguson and Carlos decided that it would be a great chance to see Cristiano in action, and hopefully complete the deal to sign him.

'A lot of clubs have made offers,' Jorge told them the night before the match. 'What can you offer Cristiano that the others can't?'

'He will play a lot of football for us and we will look after him,' Ferguson answered confidently. He had a great reputation for developing talent.

Jorge felt that it would be the perfect move for his young player, and Cristiano was delighted, too. He had been watching Manchester United on TV for years and it would be a dream come true to play for the club. They needed to agree a transfer fee but otherwise, the deal was done.

Cristiano couldn't wait for the big game. He wasn't going to let his new superstar teammates like Ryan Giggs, Rio Ferdinand and Ruud van Nistelrooy visit Portugal without learning his name. But it was Ferguson that he wanted to impress the most.

'I'm going to show off every trick in my collection,' he told his teammate, Toñito, as they warmed up.

'Well, you've got a lot of them,' the Spaniard replied. 'Will ninety minutes be enough? I guess I won't expect to get much time on the ball today!'

John O'Shea was United's right-back for the match. He looked at Sporting's left-winger, with blonde streaks in his hair, colourful boots and 'Ronaldo' on his back, and thought, 'This kid really thinks he's amazing!' He was tall but he was skinny, so O'Shea wasn't worried – he thought he could use his strength to keep him quiet.

He was wrong. Cristiano was fast, fearless, and much stronger than he looked. He made great runs behind the defence and, every time he got the ball, he dribbled forward at top speed. His control was brilliant and his feet seemed to move at a million miles an hour. O'Shea didn't know what to do. If he tried to push Cristiano out wide, the player didn't mind: he used his left foot and ran up the wing. And if he tried to push him infield, that too was fine: he just used his right foot instead.

'Rio!' O'Shea shouted. He was having a nightmare. 'I need more help here!'

Cristiano's teammates gave the ball to him as much as possible, and his clever pass helped to create Sporting's first goal. He was just too hot to handle. As he flicked the ball past O'Shea again, the only thing the defender could do was foul him.

'Come on, Sheasy!' Paul Scholes shouted. 'Get tight to him. What's going on?'

'It's not my fault,' he replied. 'This kid's unbelievable!'

With each trick Cristiano did, the crowd roared. United had won all of their pre-season matches but Sporting were making their players look like fools.

Giggs was a substitute for United and he had been looking forward to a quiet rest on the bench. But as soon as Cristiano started showing his skills, he was wide awake and watching carefully. He knew a wing wizard when he saw one.

'Wow! Who is that?' he asked Queiroz.

The assistant manager smiled. 'That's Cristiano Ronaldo.'

At half-time, the United players were shocked and exhausted. It was a long time since they had been outclassed by one player like that. Cristiano was running the show and there was nothing that any of them could do about it.

'We've got to sign him, boss,' Roy Keane said.

'Don't worry – it's all sorted,' Ferguson told him.

In the second half, Cristiano carried on his masterclass, but Ferguson wasn't watching any more. He was too busy making sure that the star became a United player.

'We're not leaving this country until we sign that boy,' he told Carlos.

'Good, I was hoping you would say that!' his assistant said.

Real Madrid had offered £8 million, so United offered £9 million. In the end, they paid over £12 million because they didn't want to fight against other clubs. Sporting asked to keep Cristiano for another season but Ferguson didn't want to wait.

'Cristiano is ready to play for us now,' he told them.

In the end, the Portuguese club couldn't compete with the money and history of Manchester United. It was sad for them to see him leave so early in his career, but it was time for Cristiano to move on.

'We're nearly there!' Ferguson whispered to Carlos.

After the match, the United players showered and ate dinner, but then the coach taking them home sat outside the stadium for ages.

'Why haven't we left yet?' Ferdinand asked. 'I want to go home!'

'They're signing Ronaldo,' Giggs replied.

'Oh OK – that's worth the wait!'

CHAPTER 12

EARLY DAYS AT OLD TRAFFORD

'This is the life!' Cristiano said, relaxing in his chair. Manchester United had booked a private jet to take him and his family to Manchester. 'Mum, I always said that once I started playing professional football, you would never have to work again. I was right!'

Dolores smiled. 'Thank you! There's still a lot of hard work ahead but I'm so proud of you, son.'

When they landed in England, Ferguson showed Cristiano the training facilities at Carrington. All of the pitches were perfect and the gym was huge with all the latest equipment.

'Can I just live here?' he joked. 'This place is better than a hotel!'

On the tour, they bumped into John O'Shea. He was still recovering from Cristiano's magic spell, but he was very happy to see that the winger would be a teammate rather than an opponent in the future.

'When are you going to pay me for my acting performance?' O'Shea joked. 'Without me, you might not be here!'

Cristiano didn't speak any English but when it was translated, he smiled. He was glad that the United players had a good sense of humour.

Once he had signed his contract, Cristiano got ready to go back to Portugal. 'So will I be leaving Sporting at the end of next season?' he asked.

Ferguson shook his head. 'No, you're joining Manchester United now.'

Cristiano was surprised. 'But I didn't even bring a suitcase! I don't have any clothes.'

'Don't worry – you can go back to Lisbon to collect your things later this week.'

First, Cristiano had to be presented to the media, along with United's other new signing, the Brazilian midfielder Kléberson.

'So what number would you like to wear?' Ferguson asked him on the way to Old Trafford.

'I wore 28 at Sporting,' Cristiano said. 'Is that available?'

'Yes it is, but I have a better idea,' his new manager replied. 'I want you to wear the Number 7!'

Cristiano had only just arrived at United but everyone knew about the amazing players that had worn the club's famous Number 7 shirt: David Beckham, George Best, Eric Cantona – and now Cristiano.

'Are you sure?'

Ferguson laughed. 'I can see that you're pretty sure of your own ability! So I think you can deal with the pressure.'

It was true. Most United youngsters were shy and respectful when they started training with legends like Giggs, Keane and Scholes. But not Cristiano. He arrived at training wearing flashy clothes and looking as confident as ever. He treated the senior players like equals.

'It's a good thing that we know how good he is,'

Gary Neville said. 'Otherwise, he wouldn't last a day here!'

The United players loved to make fun of each other and play practical jokes. Cristiano was very vain and so he was an obvious victim right from the start. His teammates made sure that he didn't get too big for his boots.

'Did you pay money for that jumper? It's a shocker!'

'This is a training ground not a night club, Ronnie!'

'Can't you get jeans in a bigger size in Portugal?'

'Those blonde streaks in your hair have got to go!'

'Becks says you can wear his shirt until he comes back!'

Cristiano accepted all of the jokes – they wouldn't be laughing so hard when he became the best player in the world. He didn't change anything: his clothes, his haircut or his self-belief. He had his own style that he loved and that was all that mattered.

In training, he never stopped showing off his skills. Cristiano watched lots of videos on the internet and then practiced the tricks until he could do them perfectly. It was entertaining, but sometimes it went too far. If he tried to do a sixth stepover in a row, Scholesy or Keano would clatter into him.

'He'll learn his lesson,' Ferguson said to himself as he watched from the sidelines. His young star didn't complain; he just got up and carried on.

Cristiano was hoping to go back to Lisbon to collect his stuff but his manager had big news for him, saying, 'You're on the bench for our game against Bolton.'

Cristiano was delighted. There was a very strong chance that he would get to play in United's very first game of the season.

Giggsy scored a great free kick, but after sixty minutes it was still only 1–0. The Old Trafford crowd wanted more and Cristiano was desperate to impress the fans. Finally, he got the call to warm up.

He could feel the adrenaline building as he did his final stretches. He was wearing silver boots for the special occasion and he was ready to let his quick feet dazzle. As he ran onto the pitch, the supporters stood up and clapped.

'Let's give them something to really cheer about!' Cristiano said to himself.

His first couple of dribbles weren't successful but he was just warming up. Then Keano passed to him on the left and he ran at the right-back. A second defender came across but Cristiano danced through both of them. The United fans were up on their feet to celebrate a second goal but just as he entered the penalty area, Cristiano slipped.

'Unlucky, but keep going,' Giggsy said. 'Their defence is terrified of you!'

Cristiano made a run towards goal and Keano threaded a great pass through to him. But as he entered the box, a player pulled him to the floor. Penalty!

'Brilliant work, Ronnie!' Keano shouted, clapping him on the back.

Ruud's spot-kick was saved but, thanks to Cristiano, United were on fire. Every time he got the ball, he moved forward to start another attack. He was too quick and skilful for Bolton. The fans loved him and so did the commentators on TV:

Sensational!

This kid's got it all!

His cross helped set up Giggsy's second and by the final whistle, it was 4–0.

'What a debut!' Scholesy cheered. 'If you can do that in thirty minutes, what can you do in ninety?'

Cristiano couldn't wait to show the whole world the answer.

CHAPTER 13

ENGLISH LESSONS

'Ref, that's a dive!' Gary Kelly shouted, as Cristiano fell to the ground in the Leeds United penalty area. 'I didn't touch him!'

'No, that's a penalty!' Cristiano screamed.

Graham Poll shook his head and waved play on. Cristiano had only been playing in the Premier League for a couple of months but he already had a reputation for going down too easily.

A few minutes later, he dribbled at Kelly again, and again he fell to the floor in the box.

'Penalty!' Cristiano screamed once more.

But as he looked up, the referee showed him a yellow card for diving. Cristiano couldn't believe it.

'What can I do?' he asked Ferguson after the match. 'It's a foul!'

'You've got to be stronger and stay on your feet more,' his manager told him. 'Football is more physical here than in the rest of Europe.'

After such a bright start against Bolton, Cristiano was struggling. He was still using his skills to beat defenders but the United players and fans wanted a better final product: goals.

'What's the point of all his tricks if we don't score at the end?' Ruud moaned. 'Whenever Becks got the ball, he crossed it and I was in the box ready for the header. But when Ronnie gets it, he dribbles for ages and I don't know if he's ever going to cross it.'

'He just needs more time,' Giggsy said, defending Cristiano. 'He's still only eighteen, so he just wants to show off. He'll learn.'

Cristiano was in the best place to learn. With Gary playing behind him on the right and Keano next to him in midfield, he didn't get away with anything. If he forgot to mark the left-back, they told him straight away. And even when United were thrashing teams, he still wasn't allowed to waste the ball by doing too many stepovers.

'What was that?' Gary shouted at him. 'How many times do I have to tell you? We're here to win!'

'But it's already 4–0!' Cristiano argued.

'It doesn't matter – 5–0 is better than 4–0. That's how we think at United.'

His teammates were hard on him because they knew how much potential he had. Cristiano was so talented, but he needed to start playing for the team, rather than just for himself. If they could get the best out of him, United could win every trophy.

'Remember, it's all about goals and assists,' Rio told him before every match. 'You don't get points for skills.'

Cristiano listened carefully to all of the advice but it wasn't easy to change his natural style. Since his childhood playing street football in Madeira, his tricks had been his main weapon. He loved to entertain and in Portugal he was able to do that and win matches at the same time. In England, that was more difficult.

'The defenders kick me all day long,' he complained to his mum. 'How can I create goals when they keep hurting me?'

'In Funchal, what did you do if someone fouled you?' Dolores asked.

'I found a way to get past them and score,' Cristiano replied.

'Exactly! You have to be clever.'

It was a mixed first season in the Premier League for Cristiano. He scored his first goal for the club with an amazing free kick against Portsmouth, but he also got his first red card for the club when he kicked the ball away in anger against Aston Villa.

'Who do you think you are?' Ferguson shouted at him in the dressing room afterwards. He was a father figure for Cristiano – he looked after him but he also taught him important lessons when he needed to. 'You've let the team down because you only care about yourself!'

Every time his manager told him off, Cristiano wiped away his tears and bounced back. It was all part of becoming a better player. He worked harder than ever with the United fitness coach, Valter di Salvo. His whole body ached and the sweat dripped down his face but he never gave up. He was adding more muscle in his chest and arms to battle against defenders, and more power in his legs to accelerate past them.

'That's it!' Di Salvo cheered after another exhausting session in the gym. 'You're becoming a proper athlete now.'

Cristiano also worked on his shooting. When training finished, he took a bag of footballs and asked one of the goalkeepers to practise with him.

'I'll just take a few free kicks,' he said, but Tim Howard knew that Cristiano was lying.

'You said that last week and we were out here for hours!'

'OK, as soon as I score three, we'll stop.'

'That will take at least two hours!' Tim joked.

Cristiano gave him a confident smile. 'No way, my shooting is getting better. I'll score!'

He took five steps back and one step across. As he ran forward, he hit the ball as hard as he could with the top of his foot, right on the valve where you pumped the ball up. It swerved through the air and dipped under Tim's diving arm at the last second. Half an hour later, Cristiano had scored fifty free kicks.

'Can we stop now?' Tim pleaded. 'They've probably locked the gates!'

'Just three more, I promise,' Cristiano said. 'I need to do it to become the best player in the world.'

United finished third in the Premier League and they made it to the FA Cup Final against Millwall. Cristiano had the chance to win his first-ever professional trophy and he was determined to end his first year on a high. As he walked out onto the pitch at the Millennium Stadium in Cardiff, he focused on Rio's message – 'goals and assists'.

At the end of the first half, United moved the ball across the field from the left to the right. When it came to Gary, he crossed into the penalty area. Cristiano made a run from the wing to the back post just in time to head the ball past the goalkeeper.

Gooooooooooooooooooooooooooooooooaaaaaaaaaaa aaaaaaaalllllllllllllllllllllllllllll!!!!!!!!!!!!!!!!!

In a flash, Cristiano's shirt was off and he ran to the fans to celebrate. 'Come on!' he roared. It was a real relief to be the Manchester United hero, rather than the villain.

At the final whistle, the Red Devils were 3–0 winners. Cristiano jumped up and down with his arms around the other United players as Keano lifted the trophy. It was a great feeling to be a key part of a successful team.

CHAPTER 14

FINDING HIS FEET

'Welcome home! It's good to see you again,' Rui Jorge said as the players arrived at Portugal's training camp for Euro 2004. Cristiano was glad to see a friendly face from his time at Sporting. He was still quite nervous around his heroes Luis Figo and Rui Costa.

'How's England?' Rui Jorge asked.

'The weather is awful!' was Cristiano's immediate reply. 'I think I've only seen one hour of sun all year. It's good to be back!'

Portugal were the host nation and they had a very strong squad for the tournament, with a good mix of experience and youth. They had never won an international trophy before but hopes were high across the country.

Cristiano was just as excited as everyone else. At nineteen, he wasn't yet in the starting eleven but he was determined to be a super-sub.

In the first match against Greece, he came on at half-time. Portugal were losing 1–0 and he was desperate to make a difference. Two Greek players ran forward and Cristiano chased after them. He was fresh and full of energy. But as the striker entered the penalty area, Cristiano couldn't stop himself in time and he clipped his ankle. Penalty!

He sat on the ground with his head in his hands – it was the worst possible start. But Cristiano worked extra hard to try to make up for his mistake and in the last minute of the match, he jumped high to head Luis's corner into the net.

Goooooooooooooooooooooooooooooaaaaaaaaaaaaaaa aaaaaaaaaaaaalllllllllllllllllllllllllllllllllllll!!!!!!!!!!!!!!!!

It was too late to save the day but Cristiano was impressing the manager, Luiz Felipe Scolari. Against Russia, he came on and set up a goal for Rui Costa.

'I hope I start against Spain,' he told his mum on the phone.

'I'm sure you will,' Dolores replied. 'They need you out there from the beginning!'

Cristiano did start the match and Portugal won 1–0. In the quarter-finals they were drawn against England.

'Great, I can't wait to play against Gary and Scholesy!' he said to Luis.

'You train with them every day,' Luis replied. 'You need to give us all of your secret information!'

After 120 minutes of tense football, the match went to penalties. Cristiano was still on the pitch and he wasn't afraid of anything.

'I'll take one,' he told Scolari confidently.

With his teammates watching from the halfway line, he made the long walk towards the penalty spot. Cristiano felt as calm as ever. He placed the ball down and slowly stepped back. He focused on the goal in front of him and fired the ball into the top left corner. Then he jogged back to his teammates with a big smile on his face.

'You make it look so easy,' Rui Jorge said.

'It *is* easy!' Cristiano replied, as his teammates celebrated the victory around him.

In the semi-final against Holland, he scored a clever header to give Portugal the lead and they held on to win 2–1.

'We're in the final!' Cristiano cheered. He was having the time of his life.

Their opponents were Greece, the team that had beaten them in their first match. Portugal wanted revenge but things didn't go according to plan. They went 1–0 down and Cristiano and the team just couldn't find an equaliser.

At the final whistle, he cried and cried. His teammates tried to comfort him but they couldn't stop the tears. Cristiano hated losing and this was the most painful defeat of his career so far.

'You'll be back to win this tournament soon,' Scolari told him, putting an arm around his shoulder.

Cristiano was still upset when he returned to England, but he had a new Premier League season to focus on. Unfortunately, it was the same old story:

'Pass the ball!'

'Cross it!'

'Stop being so selfish!'

He wasn't scoring enough goals and he wasn't creating enough goals either. There were lots of doubts and questions. Was he a winger or a striker? Could he fit into United's 4–4–2 formation? Did he fit into the United style at all? There were flashes of brilliance but he wasn't a consistent player yet.

'I'm trying my best!' Cristiano told Carlos at the end of the 2004–05 season. He was watching all of his performances on video to try and improve his game. He didn't know what more he could do.

'I know you are and you're getting better,' his assistant manager replied. 'Keep working hard and everything will soon fall into place.'

Cristiano was in Russia with the Portugal squad when he heard a knock at his hotel room door. It was Scolari and Luis. When he saw their faces, he knew that something bad had happened.

'Cristiano. You should sit down, as I have some bad news. I'm so sorry, but your father has died,' Scolari told him.

Cristiano sat on his bed in silence. He was too

shocked to say anything, or show any emotion. He loved his dad very much and he couldn't believe the news.

'I think you should go home to be with your family,' Scolari told him.

Cristiano thought about it but he decided to stay. 'No, I want to play football,' he said. It was the best form of escape and the thing he loved most. He knew it's what his father would have wanted.

For months, Cristiano found it very hard to focus on his career, but slowly his competitive spirit returned. His dad's death showed him how important it was to make the most of every moment. It was time to show the Premier League that he wasn't just a one-trick pony.

Against Bolton, Wayne Rooney dribbled into the box and passed the ball across goal. Cristiano sprinted in from the wing and tapped it past the goalkeeper.

'That's more like it, Ronnie!' Wayne shouted as they celebrated together.

'Thanks, Wazza!' he replied. They were starting to form a great partnership in attack.

In the last minute of the match, Cristiano ran at the left-back. He did one stepover, then another and then another. The defender was dizzy from watching his quick feet dance. Cristiano cut inside and struck a left foot shot into the bottom corner.

Goooooooooooooooooooooooooooooaaaaaaaaaaaaa aaaaaaaaaaaalllllllllllllllllllllllllllllllllllllllll!!!!!!!!!!!!

The United fans were on their feet, clapping and cheering. They loved watching him at his best.

His confidence was back and the goals kept coming: two against Fulham, two against Portsmouth, one against Charlton, and one against Wigan in the League Cup Final.

'Wow, you're playing like a superstar now!' Ferguson told him as United celebrated winning another trophy.

Cristiano was still dribbling at defenders and doing tricks but he was making better decisions about when to pass and when to shoot. He had found the all-important final product – goals and assists.

Cristiano was on the verge of greatness.

CHAPTER 15

ENEMY NUMBER ONE

'I'm sorry, Wazza,' Cristiano said, standing outside the England dressing room. He was still sweating from the match but he needed to make things right as quickly as possible. 'I didn't want it to end like that but I did what I had to do in order to win.'

At the 2006 World Cup in Germany, Portugal had just beaten England on penalties in the quarter-finals again, and Cristiano had played a key part in getting his Manchester United teammate sent off. When Wayne hurt the defender Ricardo Carvalho, Cristiano ran over to complain to the referee. Wayne pushed him away and so did his other United teammates, Rio and Gary, but the England superstar was soon shown a red card.

'I understand,' Wayne replied, although he was still furious. He couldn't help feeling betrayed by his friend. 'In the first half, I tried to get you booked for diving.'

'But what about that wink?' Rio asked. When Wayne left the pitch, Cristiano had winked at one of the Portugal coaches. 'That wasn't cool! Was your plan to wind Wazza up from the start?'

'No, I promise it wasn't!' Cristiano replied. 'The coach wanted me to move further forward and so I winked to say yes.'

Rio nodded. They all needed to move on fast before it caused problems at United.

'Well, the fans are going to give you a lot of stick for a while,' Wayne explained. 'We need to act like everything is normal between us but it will be a difficult summer for you.'

Portugal lost in the semi-finals to France and Cristiano's tournament was over. He was named as one of the best young players at the World Cup but that didn't make him feel much better. After a short holiday, he was scared to return to Manchester. He had seen English people wearing 'I Hate Ronaldo'

T-shirts on the internet, and there were angry letters waiting for him.

'I don't know if I can go back,' he said to Jorge. 'Do I have any other options?'

'Real Madrid and Barcelona are both interested if you decide that you have to leave,' his agent replied. 'But I think you should stay.'

Cristiano knew that it would be much easier to leave Manchester behind and make a fresh start in Spain. But Ferguson flew to Portugal to change his mind.

'I know you, kid, and I know how brave you are,' his manager told him. 'You left Madeira when you were twelve and you left Portugal when you were eighteen. If you walk away now, that's the opposite of brave. Don't do it!'

'After his red card against Argentina in 1998, Becks was enemy number one in England,' Ferguson continued. 'It was awful! But he didn't run away and soon everything went back to normal. You have to be mentally tough to be a top player and I know you have that toughness.'

In the end, Cristiano chose to stay and carry

on being brave. He was a strong character and he needed to show it at Old Trafford more than ever. With the club's support, he was going to prove his critics wrong.

He chatted with Wayne and they were soon friends again.

'Ronnie, we both want the same thing,' his teammate said. 'We want to win the Premier League and if we work together, we can do it!'

The United players made lots of jokes to make sure that there wasn't any tension in the squad.

'I'll leave these boxing gloves here,' Giggsy said, laughing, 'just in case you two need them!'

In a happy, confident dressing room, Cristiano was ready for his breakthrough season. He followed a very professional daily routine: early nights and early mornings, a healthy diet with no alcohol or fatty foods, and a bit of cycling or swimming in the evenings before bed. He was no longer the skinny show-off that he had been when he first arrived in English football. He was older, better, faster and stronger.

With exciting young talents like Cristiano and Wayne, plus experienced professionals like Giggsy, Scholesy, Gary and Rio, United finally had the recipe for success again.

'Chelsea had better watch out,' Gary, the captain, warned. 'We want the Premier League trophy back!'

As Cristiano walked out onto the pitch for the first match of the season, the Fulham fans booed. He knew that he would have to get used to that.

'Just ignore it,' Scholesy said to him. 'We've got a job to do!'

United were 3–0 up after just fifteen minutes. Wayne got the ball on the left wing and looked up. Cristiano was making a run down the right wing and he was calling for the ball. Wayne's cross was perfect and Cristiano calmly placed his shot past the goalkeeper.

Goooooooooooooooooooooooaaaaaaaaaaaaaaaaaa aaaaaaalllllllllllllllllllllllllllllllllllllllll!!!!!!!!!!!!!!!!!!

As he ran to the fans, Gary gave him a big hug. All was forgiven. It was such a relief that everything had calmed down. Now they could all focus on winning trophies. They were united again.

'Thanks – that's teamwork!' Cristiano shouted to Wayne as they celebrated the goal together.

In the second half, Cristiano passed to Wes Brown on the overlap. Wes crossed to Wayne, who put it in the bottom corner. It was 5–1! United were playing brilliant, simple football.

'It's going to be an amazing season!' Wayne predicted.

CHAPTER 16

PREMIER LEAGUE CHAMPIONS

Cristiano and Wayne formed a great partnership, as the 2006–07 season got underway. If one wasn't playing so well, the other stepped up to score the goals. And when they were both playing well, United were absolutely unstoppable.

'This is our best ever start to a Premier League season!' Gary told his teammates after a 3–1 victory over City in the Manchester derby. Cristiano and Wayne were both on the scoresheet again. 'We're nine points clear at the top and it's not even Christmas yet!'

Against Aston Villa, Wayne was left on the bench. Cristiano would have to shine on his own and he was ready for the responsibility. Opposition fans still booed him and opposition players still tried to foul him, but that only made him more determined to succeed. In the first half, he created chance after chance, but every time he shot wide or the goalkeeper made a good save.

'It's just a matter of time before we score,' Ferguson told his team at half-time. 'Keep attacking and keep shooting!'

Cristiano was happy to obey. He got the ball in his own half and dribbled at the Villa defenders. He was too quick for the first two and too skilful for the next two. When he was flying forward, he was impossible to play against. On the edge of the penalty area, Cristiano hit a shot but it was blocked. The rebound landed at his feet and he smashed it into the top corner.

Goooooooooooooooooooooooooooooooaaaaaaaaaaaaa aaaaaaaaaaaalllllllllllllllllllllllllllllllllllllllllllll!!!!!!!!!!!

Cristiano pumped his fists and then stood in front of the fans with his hands on his hips. He was in the best form of his life and everything felt so easy.

'Great goal, Ronnie!' Rio shouted as he ran over to hug the hero.

In the last week of December, Cristiano scored six goals in three games. Some of them were beautiful goals but some were simple tap-ins.

'Wow, you're becoming a top finisher!' Ole Gunnar Solskjaer told him. 'I thought you were a winger at first but you definitely have a striker's ability to get into the right place at the right time.'

'Thanks!' Cristiano said. It was nice to be praised by one of Manchester United's most famous goalscorers.

Not only was he scoring more goals than ever, he was also scoring really important goals. The Premiership was a two-horse race at the top. United were ahead of Chelsea but they couldn't afford to drop many points. Away at Fulham, the Red Devils were drawing 1–1 with a few minutes to go.

'Come on, there's still time to win this!' Rio shouted from the back.

Cristiano got the ball on the left wing and ran towards goal. A defender slid in for the tackle but he skipped away with ease. The United fans were up on their feet – could Cristiano be their hero again? As he entered the penalty area, another defender came across to stop him. In the past, he would have done a few stepovers, so that the defender backed away and waited for his tricks. Instead, Cristiano fired a quick, low shot into the bottom corner.

Goooooooooooooooooooooooooooooaaaaaaaaaaa aaaaaaaaaaaalllllllllllllllllllllllllllllllllllllll!!!!!!!!!!!!!!!

He was the matchwinner! Cristiano pointed and ran towards the Manchester United bench. With such amazing team spirit, they never gave up. Giggsy jumped on his back and so did Rio. Soon, Cristiano was in the middle of a massive team hug. Everyone knew what a crucial victory it was.

'I take back everything bad that I've ever said about you,' Gary said with a huge smile on his face. 'You're the real deal now!'

United were closing in on the title but they needed another three points in the Manchester derby. There was an incredible atmosphere at the City of Manchester Stadium, with City fans waving their blue-and-white scarves above their heads. They were desperate to stop their local rivals from winning the league.

Cristiano was used to other fans booing him and shouting abuse. It didn't faze him. Nothing fazed him. He was determined to win the Premier League.

Early in the match, Cristiano was tackled and as he fell to the ground, City defender Michael Ball stamped on his chest. Cristiano rolled around in agony but the referee hadn't seen it. When he was younger, he might have done something silly but now he was more mature.

'Don't worry, I'll get my revenge by scoring a goal,' Cristiano told Wayne as he got back to his feet.

Later in the first half, Cristiano got the ball on the right side of the penalty area. He was one-on-one with Ball, his favourite game. The defender was in big trouble now. He did one stepover, then another. As he moved the ball to the right, Ball stuck out his foot. Penalty!

Cristiano took the spot-kick himself. The City fans behind the goal stood up and tried to put him off but he coolly sent the goalkeeper the wrong way and placed a perfect shot right in the corner.

Goooooooooooooooooooooooooooooooaaaaaaaaaaaa aaaaaaaaaaalllllllllllllllllllllllllllllllllllll!!!!!!!!!!!!!!!!

As he walked back for the restart, Cristiano didn't smile. It wasn't over yet. It was only when the final whistle went that he allowed himself to relax. Chelsea had to beat Arsenal the next day, or United would be champions.

'Go on, Arsenal!' Cristiano shouted at the TV.

He was watching the game at home with his brother-in-law, Zé. When it finished 1–1, they hugged.

'We've won the league!' Cristiano cheered. He couldn't wait to lift the trophy.

The celebrations came on the final day of the season at Old Trafford. United lost 1–0 to West Ham but it didn't matter. The fans held up banners that said 'We Got Our Trophy Back!' and 'Ronaldo: The Best in the World'.

It was the best day of Cristiano's life. Wearing

a Portugal flag as a cape, he ran around spraying champagne all over his teammates. Together, they had achieved their dream.

Campeones, campeones, olé olé olé.

Cristiano was very happy to share his special moment with his mum. Dolores joined him on the pitch and they waved to the fans. They had been through a lot but it had all been worth it.

'What a season!' Dolores said, wiping away her tears. She was so proud of her son. Cristiano had won the Premier League, and the PFA Player of the Year and Young Player of the Year awards too.

'I know, but we can do better,' he replied. There was always room for improvement. 'I want the Champions League trophy next!'

CHAPTER 17

THE DOUBLE

'So you want to be the best player in the world?'
René Meulensteen, the United first-team coach
asked Cristiano. He was suspended for three
matches after a red card against Portsmouth, so
they had some time to work on individual training.
As always, Cristiano was hungry to learn new
things.

He nodded eagerly. That had been his big aim
since the age of five.

'OK, well I can definitely help you with that,'
Meulensteen replied.

Together, they looked at all of Cristiano's strengths
and weaknesses. They agreed that his technique,

his strength, his speed and his work rate were all excellent.

'OK, now for the negatives,' Meulensteen continued. 'You're not as bad as you used to be but I still think you could be even less selfish. When you do a bit of skill, think about it – am I doing this to make myself look good, or is it really helping the team?'

Cristiano thought back to Rio's 'goals and assists' message – yes, he still had work to do.

'You need to set some big targets for this season,' his coach suggested. 'You scored twenty-three goals last season.'

'Yes, that was my best total ever,' Cristiano boasted proudly.

'OK, but you can score a lot more. Remember, they don't have to be wonder goals every time! How many goals are you aiming for this season?'

He thought about it for a minute. 'I can get to thirty goals at least.'

Meulensteen shook his head. 'No, you have to aim higher than that. I want you to score over forty!'

Cristiano practised striking the ball in different

ways for different situations: when he was shooting near the goal, when he was shooting from a wide angle, and when he was shooting from a long way away.

'Did you really need to control the pass there?' Meulensteen asked him. 'You could have hit that one first time!'

'Which corner are you going to aim for this time?' he always asked Cristiano in advance.

'Bottom left!' he said and he pictured the ball hitting the back of the net. When the pass came, he placed it exactly where he had imagined.

'Good!' Meulensteen shouted, clapping Cristiano's progress.

The sessions were a huge success. By February, he had already scored twenty-seven goals.

'What did I tell you?' his coach said with a smile. 'Forty is your target now!'

But after a couple of poor team performances, United slipped to second in the Premier League table. Cristiano couldn't do it all on his own.

'That wasn't good enough!' Ferguson screamed at

his players after a derby defeat to Manchester City. 'We're throwing the title away!'

There was no way that Cristiano was going to let that happen. He was hungry for more trophies and he urged his teammates to work harder and play better. He led by example with nine goals in his next eight league games, and United fought their way back to the top. Ferguson even gave him the captain's armband against Bolton.

'Thanks, boss!' Cristiano said before kick-off. 'I won't let you down!'

He scored both goals in a 2–0 win. He enjoyed his new central Number 10 role, which meant he got even more of the ball. Cristiano loved being at the centre of everything.

United beat Arsenal and Chelsea to the 2007–08 Premier League title but there was still one question that Cristiano needed to answer – could he play his best football in the biggest matches? To be the best in the world, he had to be brilliant on the biggest stage.

'He went missing in last year's FA Cup Final and the Champions League semi-final against AC Milan too,' his critics argued. 'He's been amazing this season but let's wait and see. It's one thing scoring goals against Bolton and Portsmouth, but he's never scored against Chelsea!'

'Challenge accepted,' Cristiano told himself.

In the Champions League, his performances were hit-and-miss. In the quarter-final against Roma, Scholesy crossed to the back post and Cristiano sprinted thirty yards to power an incredible header past the goalkeeper.

'That's one of the best headers I've ever seen!' Wayne shouted as they celebrated the goal. Cristiano had jumped so high that he hurt himself when he came back down to earth.

But then in the semi-final against Barcelona, Cristiano was quiet and missed a penalty. In the final against Chelsea, United would need him at his best.

'I want you to keep running at the Chelsea defenders,' Ferguson told him before kick-off in Moscow. 'They'll be terrified of your pace and power.'

Cristiano was desperate to be the hero, but it was

a very tight game and he couldn't find much space to work his magic. Then midway through the first half, Wes put a cross into the box. Cristiano was at the back post and he leaped into the air, just like he had against Roma. He directed his header perfectly into the bottom corner.

Goooooooooooooooooooooooooooooaaaaaaaaaaaaaaa aaaaaaaaaaalllllllllllllllllllllllllllllllllllllllll!!!!!!!!!!!!!!

Cristiano pumped his fist and jumped into the air. He had scored a big goal in the biggest game. His teammates jumped on him.

'That's what we needed from you!' Rio shouted. 'Now, let's have some more!'

That wasn't easy when the defence was watching him so closely. Whenever he got the ball, Ricardo Carvalho fouled him. Chelsea scored an equaliser and the match went to extra time and then to penalties.

'I'll take one,' Cristiano told Ferguson. He had been United's penalty taker all season.

When it was his turn, he picked up the ball and kissed it for good luck. He placed it down on the spot and then stepped back and took a long, deep breath with his hands on his hips. He was ready.

He paused a few times in his run-up but the goalkeeper wasn't fooled. Petr Cech stood up tall and then dived to his right to make the save.

Cristiano put his hands to his face and then looked down at the pitch. He had taken a poor penalty at the worst possible moment. Had he lost the final for his team? He walked slowly back to the halfway line and watched with his teammates.

When Edwin van der Sar saved Nicolas Anelka's penalty to win the shootout, Cristiano fell down on the grass. There were so many emotions running through his body: fear, sadness, relief, joy. He lay down in the centre circle and cried.

'Get up, we've won!' Gary shouted to him eventually.

The party went on for hours. The rain was pouring down but Cristiano didn't care. He had a Champions League winner's medal around his neck and that was the best feeling in the world.

CHAPTER 18

THE REAL DEAL

'I'm the best player in the world now!' Cristiano told his United teammates as they prepared for another Premier League season. By now, they were used to his self-belief – and his total lack of modesty.

'You think you're better than Messi?' Wayne asked. He knew that question would wind Cristiano up.

'Of course!' he replied. 'Last season, I won the Premier League *and* the Champions League. What more can I do? And I scored forty-two goals, whereas he only scored sixteen.'

Everything was a competition for Cristiano and in December 2008, he was confirmed as the winner of the Ballon d'Or, the award given to the world's best player each year. As he sat in the front row at the ceremony, he was confident that Brazilian legend Pelé would announce his name.

'Cristiano Ronaldo!'

He walked onto the stage and the players and coaches clapped and cheered. What a feeling! When Pelé presented him with the trophy, he couldn't stop smiling. After years of hard work, he had reached the very top of the game. They showed a video of his best goals and then it was time for him to make a speech:

'This is another amazing and emotional moment for me. I want to dedicate this award to my family, my friends and my teammates. I couldn't have done any of this without them.'

But Cristiano had no plans to relax after achieving his dream. 'Tomorrow, I will wake up and try to become even better,' he told the media that night. 'The best is yet to come!'

Ferguson was very pleased for Cristiano, but he was worried that his star would soon move

elsewhere to become even better. After five years
at Old Trafford, Real Madrid were offering him lots
of money, sunshine, superstar teammates, and even
more success. How could he say no to that?

'It will be hard to keep him much longer,' Carlos
agreed. 'He came to England when he was eighteen
and at some point, he will definitely go to Spain.'

Ferguson went to visit Cristiano and they chatted
about the future. Cristiano wasn't sure that there
was anything left for him to achieve in English
football but his manager persuaded him to give it one
more year.

'If you still want to leave next summer, then we
won't stop you,' Ferguson said.

Cristiano agreed. He owed Manchester United –
the fans, the players, the coaches, the manager – one
more season. He signed a new contract at United,
but in the dressing room he was already talking
about becoming a *galáctico*.

'Don't leave!' Rio tried to persuade him every
week. 'If you stay, we can become the greatest team
in the history of Manchester United!'

As a kid, Cristiano had always wanted to play for Madrid, and his mum shared his passion. It was a club with so much history.

'I want to see my son playing for Real!' Dolores had been telling him for years.

On the pitch, Cristiano was still giving everything for United. He was determined to help the club defend their British and European titles. It was very difficult to live up to his previous amazing season but he did his best.

In the Champions League, they needed to win away against Porto to make it through to the semi-finals. After five minutes, Cristiano got the ball forty yards from goal. He took one touch to control it, one touch to move it to the right and then took a shot. Only Cristiano had the confidence to try it. The ball flew through the air like an arrow, past the goalkeeper's arm and into the top corner.

Goooooooooooooooooooooooooooooaaaaaaaaaaaaaaa aaaaaaaaaaalllllllllllllllllllllllllllllllllllllllllll!!!!!!!!!!!!!

Cristiano watched it hit the back of the net and then he turned and ran back as if he had done something normal. But it wasn't normal; it was very, very special. The United fans went wild and so did the players.

'What a strike, Ronnie!' Rio shouted as he gave him a big hug. 'You were nearly at the halfway line.'

In the semi-final against Arsenal, Cristiano set up the first goal for Ji-Sung Park and then he won a free kick out on the right. Most players would have tried to cross the ball into the box, but not Cristiano.

'I've got this,' he told Scholesy.

It was a long way from goal but he had already proved that distance wasn't a problem. He stepped back and took a long, deep breath. Cristiano pictured the ball going into the corner of the net, just as Meulensteen had taught him. His shot dipped and swerved past the Arsenal goalkeeper.

Goooooooooooooooooooooooooaaaaaaaaaaaaaaaaaa aaaaaaaaaaaaaallllllllllllllllllllllllllllllllllllllll!!!!!!!!!!!

This time, Cristiano didn't try to act cool. He ran along the touchline with this arms outstretched like the wings of an aeroplane. He nodded his head to say: 'Yes, I *am* the best!'

Everything was going to plan. United were through to the Champions League Final again and a win in the Manchester Derby would put them on the verge of a third Premier League title in a row.

After fifteen minutes, Cristiano stood over a free kick. He could see the fear on the faces of the City players. They knew exactly what he could do. His shot swerved and deflected off a player in the wall. There was nothing the goalkeeper could do to stop it.

Goooooooooooooooooooooooooooaaaaaaaaaaaaaaaaa aaaaaaaaaaaaaalllllllllllllllllllllllllllllllll!!!!!!!!!!!!!

Cristiano was the United hero yet again. What would they do without him?

'Are you sure you want to go to Spain?' Giggsy asked him. 'You'll win more trophies here and the football is more exciting.'

But Real Madrid didn't give up and neither did Cristiano. Eventually, a record transfer fee of £80 million was agreed. He had his dream move, which made him the most expensive player in the world.

But first, there was one last match to play for United: the Champions League Final against Barcelona.

'It's you against Messi tonight!' Wayne said before kick-off. He knew that Cristiano was at his best when he was feeling really competitive.

Cristiano was desperate to show the world that he was still the best player, but his right foot had been hurting for months. He did his best to create something magical but in the end, Barcelona were just too good.

'I'll just have to get my revenge as a Real player,' he told himself as he walked off the pitch at the Stadio Olimpico in Rome.

Cristiano was very grateful for everything that Manchester United had done for him over his six years there. He would miss the club very much but it was time for a big new adventure in Spain. He couldn't wait.

CHAPTER 19

LIFE AS A *GALÁCTICO*

Walking out in front of 70,000 United fans at Old Trafford was an incredible feeling, but walking out in front of 80,000 Real Madrid fans at the Bernabéu was, just maybe, even better. And Cristiano wasn't even playing a football match! He was tired and very hot in the Spanish summer sun but the atmosphere took his mind off all that. It was unbelievable. People had queued outside the stadium for hours just to see him. Cristiano was now a *galáctico*, a real superstar.

As he walked out of the tunnel and along the special carpet, the supporters cheered loudly.

Ronaldo! Ronaldo! Ronaldo!

Cristiano waved to them and gave two thumbs-ups. He was dressed in the full Real Madrid kit, the classic white. Raúl, the captain, wore his favourite Number 7 shirt and so Cristiano had chosen the Number 9. It confirmed that he was now a striker rather than a winger, and it also showed his ambition – it was the number that Real Madrid legend Alfredo di Stéfano had worn.

When he reached the stage in the middle of the pitch, Cristiano had to speak to the fans. He had prepared a few lines but with 80,000 faces waiting, he couldn't remember them. 'Wow, thank you, I'm so happy to be here!' he said with a huge smile across his face. 'I always dreamed of playing for this club and now it's a reality – I'm a Real Madrid player! *iHala Madrid!*'

The crowd roared. Next, it was time to show off his tricks. Cristiano did a few keepy-uppies with a ball and then gave it to a child nearby. It was a nice gesture and the fans loved it. Before he left the pitch, he kissed the club badge on his shirt.

'I'm going to love it here!' he said to himself.

Florentino Pérez, the new Real Madrid President, had been busy. As well as Cristiano, the club had also signed Spanish midfielder Xabi Alonso, Brazilian playmaker Kaká and French striker Karim Benzema. It was an exciting project. They were building a team to defeat Messi's Barcelona and Cristiano was the main man.

'It's time to win the title back!' he told Pepe, his Portuguese teammate. Together with the Brazilians Marcelo and Kaká, they quickly formed a close group of friends. This really helped Cristiano to settle into a new club in a new city in a new country.

He wasn't the team leader straight away, but just like at United, he made sure that he was in charge of all the set pieces – corners, free kicks, and penalties too. In his first La Liga match, he stepped up and placed a perfect spot-kick in the bottom corner.

Goooooooooooooooooooooooooooaaaaaaaaaaaaaaaaaa aaaaaaaaaaalllllllllllllllllllllllllllllllllllllllll!!!!!!!!!!!!!!!

Cristiano pumped his fists and roared with pride. His new teammates gathered round to congratulate him.

'This is the start of something special!' Raúl told him.

Cristiano scored five goals in his first four league matches but then disaster struck: he got an injury.

'No!' he shouted as he hobbled off the pitch. His right ankle was really painful. 'Why is this happening now? I'm just getting going!'

Cristiano found it very difficult to rest. He never liked watching football, but he really hated watching his own team play without him.

'How much longer?' he asked the physio every day. He had always worked so hard on his fitness that he very rarely got injured. Life on the sidelines was a nightmare.

As soon as possible, Cristiano was back in the gym and on the training field. He was the first in and the last out. He wanted to be in perfect shape for his comeback.

'Take it easy!' the coaches told him. 'If you're not careful, you'll injure yourself again.'

Cristiano returned just in time for his first 'El Clásico' game – as every such game between Madrid and Barcelona was called. Every time he touched the ball, the boos of the Barcelona fans filled the Nou Camp. In the first half, Kaká ran through the defence and played a great pass to Cristiano. He was one-on-one with the goalkeeper and he tried to calmly place his shot into the bottom corner. But Victor Valdés saved it with his legs.

'I should have scored that!' Cristiano screamed, with his hands on his head.

'Don't worry, Cris, the goals will come,' Xabi said encouragingly to his teammate.

But Barcelona won 1–0 and Cristiano was furious. It was his responsibility to score big goals in big games, and he had failed. Real were no longer top of the league.

'I've got to make it up to the team,' he told himself.

He was trying too hard to be the hero, and sometimes his passion got him into trouble. He scored lots of goals, but if he got frustrated, he kicked out.

'You've got to calm down,' his manager, Manuel Pellegrini, told him after he got sent off against Málaga. 'Defenders are trying to make you angry and you're falling for it every time!'

Cristiano finished his first season as Real Madrid's top scorer, with thirty-three goals. But despite his best efforts, his team finished second behind Barcelona and they didn't even make it to the quarter-finals of the

Champions League. With club legend Raúl moving to Germany, it was time for a new era.

'I didn't leave United to come here and lose!' he told Karim grumpily. 'We've got great players here but we don't have the confidence at the moment.'

Cristiano was thinking about Sir Alex and how he taught his teams never to give up until the final whistle. His players always believed they would win, no matter what. Real really needed a manager like that.

'Cris, Pellegrini has been sacked!' Karim told him a few days later.

He wasn't surprised. 'So who's replacing him?'

'The rumour is José Mourinho.'

Cristiano smiled. He knew Mourinho well. They had first met in Portugal, when Cristiano was at Sporting Lisbon and Mourinho was managing Porto. In England, when Cristiano was playing for United, Mourinho was managing Chelsea, having just won the Champions League with Inter Milan. Not everyone liked him, but 'The Special One' was certainly a born winner, just like Cristiano.

'Perfect!'

CHAPTER 20

RONALDO VS MESSI

When the referee blew the final whistle, Cristiano walked straight off the pitch and down the tunnel. He didn't want to speak to anyone – he was too angry. With Mourinho in charge and new signings Mesut Özil and Sami Khedira in midfield, Real Madrid were expected to challenge Barcelona for the La Liga title. But instead, they had just been thrashed 5–0.

'What did I tell you before kick-off?' Mourinho shouted at his players in the dressing room. 'I told you to stay calm, defend well and then get it to Cristiano on the counter-attack. But what did you do instead? You ran around like headless chickens, you got frustrated, and Cristiano barely had a touch!'

Just as Lionel Messi was the focus of the Barcelona team, Cristiano was now the focus of the Real Madrid team. He had his Number 7 shirt back and the club relied on him to be their star. Mourinho knew all about Cristiano's competitive spirit and so he used it to get the best out of him.

'Cris, Messi destroyed us today. What happened to you?'

'I was alone up front and the midfielders didn't pass the ball to me!' he argued.

'But Messi creates chances out of nothing. You need to do more!'

In the next match against Valencia, it was still 0–0 with twenty minutes to go. They needed to win to keep the pressure on Barcelona. As Mesut ran forward with the ball, Cristiano made a great run behind the right-back. When the pass arrived, he took one touch and then smashed it into the net.

Goooooooooooooooooooooooooooaaaaaaaaaaaaaaaa aaaaaaalllllllllllllllllllllllllllllllllllllllllllllll!!!!!!!!!!!!!!!!

'Cris to the rescue again!' Pepe cheered as they celebrated.

With five minutes to go, Cristiano picked up the ball just inside the opposition half. As he ran at the defenders, they backed away. On the edge of the penalty area, he did one stepover to the right, then one to the left. The tired Valencia players had no idea which way he would go. In the end, he went to the right and shot past the keeper.

Goooooooooooooooooooooooooaaaaaaaaaaaaaaaa aaaaaaaaaalllllllllllllllllllllllllllllllllllllllllll!!!!!!!!!!!!!!!!!

Cristiano stood with his arms up in the air, and nodded his head to the fans. Yes, he could still compete with Messi as the best player in the world.

By Christmas, Cristiano had eighteen league goals, one more than Messi. But Messi had won El Clásico, and Barcelona, not Real Madrid, were top of La Liga.

'I won't be happy until we are the number one team in Spain!' Cristiano told Mourinho. He also wouldn't be happy until he was the number one player again. Messi had won the Ballon d'Or in 2009 *and* 2010. The world thought that Cristiano and Lionel were bitter enemies but that wasn't true. They were full of respect for each other and when they met at awards ceremonies and matches, they often chatted happily together. It was only on the football pitch that their competitive spirits came out and they became fierce rivals. Cristiano and Messi were both so determined to be the best player in the world.

In April, Real Madrid played Barcelona four times: once in La Liga, once in the Spanish Cup, and twice in the Champions League semi-finals. Cristiano couldn't wait for the battle to begin. After a boring 1–1 draw in the league, the excitement grew for the Spanish Cup final.

'We can do this!' Cristiano shouted to his teammates. 'If we win this, we'll have the advantage for the Champions League too.'

After more than a hundred minutes of football, neither team had scored. Then Ángel Di María played a great one-two with Marcelo down the left and put a great cross into the box. Cristiano was at the back post and he used all of his strength to leap into the air and power his header into the top corner.

Goooooooooooooooooooooooooooooooaaaaaaaaaaaaaaaa aaaaaaaaaaalllllllllllllllllllllllllllllllllllllllll!!!!!!!!!!!!!!

He had done it! Cristiano slid along the grass on his knees. Finally, he was the matchwinner against Barcelona. The revenge felt so sweet.

'You're a hero now!' Sergio Ramos told him as the fans chanted his name.

A week later, Cristiano was focused on the Champions League tie. It was nice to win the Spanish Cup, but this was the one he really wanted. Even though the first leg was at home in the Bernabéu, Real Madrid didn't really attack. Mourinho didn't want to concede an important away goal.

'You've got to come up and support me!' Cristiano complained to Mesut and Ángel. He was getting more and more frustrated on his own up front.

'But the boss says we have to defend!' Mesut replied. He was just doing his job.

When Messi scored two late goals to give Barcelona the victory, Cristiano was furious.

'Why are we playing like this?' he asked Mourinho. 'We shouldn't be scared of them! We're better than them and we need to show it.'

'We play like this so that you have freedom,' his

manager told him in front of all of his teammates. It was time to teach his superstar a lesson. 'But today, we gave you freedom and you didn't create anything!'

Cristiano was upset but he knew that Mourinho was right. Instead of moaning, he had to do more to help his team. It wasn't all about him.

Messi and Cristiano both scored an amazing fifty-three goals that season, but it was Messi who won the La Liga and Champions League double.

'Next season, I won't care so much about my individual targets,' he told his mum. He wasn't giving up yet. 'It's all about the team target – we have to stop Barcelona!'

Real Madrid lost the next El Clásico 3–1 but it was their only league defeat in eight months. Cristiano was scoring goals for fun, and more importantly, Los Blancos were six points clear at the top of the table.

Against Real Sociedad, Cristiano beat the offside trap and slotted the ball past the keeper. It was his thirty-fourth league goal of the season, but it was also a landmark goal for him.

'Congratulations on your hundredth goal in La Liga!' Xabi told him as they celebrated.

'Thanks, and it only took me ninety-two matches!' he boasted. 'That's a record! It took Messi over one hundred and fifty games!'

The only thing on Cristiano's mind was beating Messi and Barcelona. The second El Clásico of the season became the biggest match of his career.

'Barcelona look weak but we are at our strongest!' Mourinho told his players. 'This is our moment!'

The atmosphere at the Nou Camp was very tense. The Barcelona fans booed Cristiano all through the game, but it didn't bother him. He was so focused on winning. After fifteen minutes, Real took the lead but Barça equalised in the second half. A draw would be enough for Madrid but it wasn't enough for Cristiano.

Ángel passed to Mesut on the right. He kept running for the one-two but Cristiano made an even better run in the middle. Mesut's pass could not have been better and Cristiano was one-on-one with

Victor Valdes again. This time, there was no way he would miss. He curled his shot into the net.

Gooooooooooooooooooooooooaaaaaaaaaaaaaaaaa aaaaaaaaaaaaallllllllllllllllllllllllllllllllll!!!!!!!!!!!!!!!!

The Madrid fans went wild but Cristiano played it cool. He didn't rip off his shirt or throw his hands up in the air. Instead, he just told everyone to calm down. He was only doing what he always did – scoring important goals.

At the final whistle, Cristiano pumped his fists, hugged his teammates and then hugged Mourinho. His tactics had worked. Cristiano had finally won the Spanish league, and he had won it by beating Messi's Barcelona!

When he lifted the trophy a few weeks later, Cristiano thought about how hard he had worked for his success. Every hour in the gym and on the training pitch had been worth it.

But with one target achieved, it was now time for another: the Champions League.

CHAPTER 21

LA DÉCIMA

'La Décima' – 'The Tenth'. Cristiano rarely went a day in Madrid without hearing that phrase. Los Blancos had won their ninth Champions League trophy way back in 2002 and the fans were desperate to win a tenth. The players could feel the pressure in every match.

'Eleven years is a long time for them to wait,' Pepe admitted. 'A club like this expects to win everything all the time!'

Real Madrid had lost in the semi-finals of the Champions League for three years in a row. The supporters were starting to think that their team was cursed.

'Yes, but I'm confident about this season,'
Cristiano told his Portuguese teammate.

'You're confident about every season!' Pepe teased
him.

Cristiano smiled. 'That's true, but I think this is
our best team yet.'

As well as Cristiano and Karim, Real Madrid now
had Isco, Luka Modric and Gareth Bale in attack.
Cristiano was still the king but it was good to have
great players around him. He couldn't do it all on
his own.

In the group stage, he scored nine goals in five
games.

'Wow, you really mean business this year, don't
you?' Karim laughed.

He really did. His great rival Messi held the record
for most goals in a Champions League season –
fourteen. Cristiano was off to a great start in the
tournament.

After years of vying with Lionel Messi for the title
of the world's best, he was reclaiming top spot again.
At the 2013 Ballon d'Or ceremony, Pelé called out

Cristiano's name just like he had five years earlier. As he thanked everyone in his life, Cristiano cried. It was another amazing and emotional day for him after a long, hard battle. They were tears of joy – he was the best player in the world again.

Isco won the ball and passed to Karim, who passed to Cristiano. He used his strength to out-muscle the defender, dribbled around the keeper and shot into the net.

Goooooooooooooooooooooooooooooaaaaaaaaaaaaa aaaaaaaaaaalllllllllllllllllllllllllllllllll!!!!!!!!!!!!!!!!!!!!

They were thrashing Schalke 6–0 with brilliant attacking football. Real Madrid, and Cristiano in particular, looked unstoppable. He was up to thirteen goals and the quarter-finals hadn't even started yet.

Their next opponents were Borussia Dortmund, the team that had knocked them out the year before. Cristiano loved revenge – it spurred him on.

Gareth got the first goal and Isco got the second. Cristiano was pleased for his teammates but he wanted to get on the scoresheet himself. In the second half, Luka won the ball and fed it to Cristiano. He calmly took it round the keeper to make it 3–0.

'We're playing like a great team!' he said, giving Luka a big hug.

In the semi-final, Real Madrid faced Bayern Munich, another team that had knocked them out of the tournament in the past. And the team's manager was the former Barcelona manager, Pep Guardiola.

'We *have* to win this!' Cristiano told his teammates. Failure was not an option.

Karim scored the only goal in the first leg at the Bernabéu. Real had the lead but they would need to play very well in Germany.

The new Madrid manager, Carlo Ancelotti, liked a more attacking style than Mourinho. He decided to play Cristiano, Karim, Gareth, Luka, Ángel *and* Xabi all in the same team away from home.

'You're crazy but I love it!' Cristiano told him. They had no reason to be scared of anyone.

Ancelotti's tactics worked. Sergio Ramos scored two headers and suddenly Bayern needed to score

three goals to beat them. As they attacked, Real
counter-attacked. Karim passed to Gareth, who
passed to Cristiano. Cristiano nutmegged the keeper.

*Goooooooooooooooooooooooooaaaaaaaaaa
aaaaaaaaaaaaaaaallllllllllllllllllllllllllllllllllllllllllllll
ll!!!!!!!!!!!!!!!*

He had his fifteenth goal of the tournament – the
record was now his! He held up both hands – ten –
and then turned one hand around to make the other
five. He did it over and over again like a dance. He
was so happy with his achievement.

'Well done, Cris!' Gareth shouted, giving him a
double high-five.

Cristiano scored again to make his tally sixteen and
Madrid were through to the Champions League final
in Lisbon. He couldn't wait for his big homecoming.

'Just one more game to win!' he reminded his
teammates.

Atlético Madrid beat Chelsea to set up an all-
Madrid final. Atlético were the La Liga champions
and they had beaten Real once and drawn with
them once. They were a very difficult team to score

against, but Cristiano was in the best goalscoring form of his life.

He wasn't 100 per cent fit, but there was no way that Cristiano would miss the Champions League Final. As he walked out of the tunnel and past the trophy, he couldn't help having a quick look. It had been six years since his triumph with Manchester United. He was just as impatient as the Real Madrid fans.

'Come on!' he roared.

But Atlético took the lead, and with seconds to go, looked like they would hold on for the victory. Cristiano took shot after shot but nothing was going in. Then in the last minute, Sergio Ramos scored a brilliant header to make it 1–1. Real could still win the final.

In extra time, they were too good for their tired opponents. Gareth made it 2–1 and then Marcelo made it 3–1. Real were the champions, but Cristiano wasn't finished. He wanted to score in the final. He dribbled at the Atlético defenders and one of them stuck out a leg. Penalty!

Cristiano picked up the ball and put it down on

the spot. He ran up and sent the goalkeeper the wrong way.

Goooooooooooooooooooooooooooooooooooaaaaaaaaa aaaaaaaaaaaaaaaaaaalllllllllllllllllllllllllllll!!!!!!!!!!!!!!!

The dream was complete. Cristiano took off his shirt and celebrated. He looked like The Incredible Hulk as he roared at the sky.

The party had already started in the stands – 'La Décima' was finally theirs. The celebrations carried on all night and continued back in Madrid at the Bernabéu a few days later. The players returned home as heroes.

It was another golden moment in a golden career. But Cristiano always wanted more.

CHAPTER 22

LA UNDÉCIMA

'I can't believe they've sacked Ancelotti,' Cristiano said to Sergio Ramos. Real Madrid needed one manager for a long time, not a different manager every year. It was difficult for the players to adapt to each new style. 'He was doing a good job!'

'I agree, but you know what it's like here,' his captain replied. 'If you don't win a trophy straight away, you're out.'

'Yes, but we have to replace him with someone really special,' Cristiano argued. 'Is Rafa Benítez the man to do it?'

'We have to give him a chance. He won the Champions League with Liverpool! We've tried

Mourinho and we've tried Ancelotti. We can't try Guardiola because he's at Barcelona – who else is there?'

Sergio Ramos was right but Cristiano wanted the very best players and coaches around him. He had won the 2014 Ballon d'Or, but in order to win it again he needed to win another major trophy – La Liga or the Champions League, or preferably both. Being the top goalscorer in Europe wasn't enough.

Away at Espanyol, he scored five goals in a game for the first time ever. Every time he scored, he performed his new favourite goal celebration. He jumped into the air and threw his arms down in the dramatic style of a bullfighter. He was showing the back of his shirt to the crowd.

'Just in case they forget my name!' Cristiano joked to Karim.

But there was no way that the Real Madrid supporters would ever forget his name. He had just gone down in history as their top La Liga goalscorer of all time.

'That's 230 goals in 203 games – unbelievable!' Pepe said, giving him a big hug.

It was a great honour but Cristiano never lost his focus on the big battle – Real Madrid vs Barcelona. Barcelona had the amazing attacking trio, 'MSN': Messi, Suárez and Neymar. But Real had an attacking trio of their own, 'BBC': Benzema, Bale and Cristiano. Who would be victorious?

When their rivals came to the Bernabéu, Messi wasn't even in the team and Barcelona still won 4–0. It was another humiliating El Clásico defeat for Real Madrid. At the final whistle, the fans booed their team and Cristiano walked off the pitch scratching his head. Something had to change, but what?

Benítez was sacked in January and he was replaced by club legend Zinedine 'Zizou' Zidane. Cristiano had a lot of respect for Zidane and Zidane had a lot of respect for Cristiano. Straight away, the new manager gave him more freedom on the pitch.

'He's the soul of Real Madrid,' Zizou told the media.

'BBC' won game after game, but in the end Barcelona won La Liga by a single point on the final day of the season. It was heartbreaking, but Real Madrid still had one game left – yet another Champions League final.

Cristiano had been the star of the tournament once again. He had scored thirteen goals before the quarter-finals – it was definitely his favourite competition!

Against Wolfsburg, Real lost the first leg 2–0. It was a big shock but Cristiano didn't panic.

'We've still got time to make this right,' he told his teammates before the second leg. 'We just need to win 3–0!'

And that's exactly what they did, with Cristiano scoring an incredible hat-trick. The first was a tap-in, the second was a flicked header and the third was a stunning free kick that swerved through the wall and into the bottom corner.

'Come on!' Cristiano shouted to the fans as they celebrated the great escape. He loved being the hero. It was the best job in the world.

In the final, Real played Madrid rivals Atlético, as they had two years before.

'We lost to them in the league in February,' Cristiano reminded his teammates before kick-off. 'If we'd won that match, we would be La Liga champions right now. Let's go out there and get our revenge!'

The Real players roared. They were determined to win their eleventh Champions League trophy, 'La Undécima'. Sergio Ramos scored after fifteen minutes but Cristiano couldn't grab a second, no matter how hard he tried. Then with ten minutes to go, Atlético scored. The Champions League final went to penalties.

Cristiano could barely walk. After 120 minutes of football, his legs had stopped working properly. But there was still one thing left for him to do.

'I'll take the last one,' Cristiano told Zidane confidently. 'I want to score the winner!'

He still had nightmares about his miss in the 2009 final for Manchester United, but it was time to replace that with a new, happy memory.

As he walked up to take his spot-kick, Cristiano

knew that Real would win the trophy if he scored. He had the chance to be the hero yet again. He stood on the edge of the penalty area and took a deep breath. Once he felt calm, he pictured the ball hitting the back of the net. Yes, he could do this.

Goooooooooooooooooooooooooooaaaaaaaaaaaaaaa aaaaaaaaaaaalllllllllllllllllllllllllllllllllll!!!!!!!!!!!!!!!!!

The goalkeeper dived the wrong way and Cristiano was a Champions League winner for the third time. What a moment! He took his shirt off and threw it in the air.

'Come on!' he shouted to the fans above him. He was soon at the bottom of a big pile of players.

Cristiano stood just behind Sergio Ramos as he lifted the trophy. He was desperate to get his hands on it. When it came to him, he held it high and gave it a shake. Then he kissed it and passed it to his Portuguese teammate, Pepe.

'Our next trophy will be Euro 2016!' Cristiano told him, with a smile.

CHAPTER 23

PROUD TO BE PORTUGUESE

'It would be so amazing to win a tournament with Portugal!' Cristiano said to former Manchester United teammate, Nani, as they prepared for Euro 2016 in France.

'Messi still hasn't won the World Cup or the Copa América with Argentina – you could beat him to it!' Nani said with a smile. He always knew that the 'M' word would make Cristiano even more determined.

Cristiano had been the captain of the national team for nearly ten years, but since losing in the Euro 2004 final to Greece, Portugal had gone backwards. Cristiano was their all-time leading goalscorer but at crucial moments, he had failed. The fans watched his amazing performances for Manchester United and Real Madrid and asked, 'When will he play like that for us?'

At Euro 2012, Cristiano had wanted to take their final penalty in the semi-final shoot-out against Spain, but it was all over before he could take it. The Portuguese people weren't happy.

'Typical!' they said. 'It's all about him, and never about the team.'

Cristiano scored a great hat-trick against Sweden to take his team to the 2014 World Cup in Brazil. However, he was injured for the tournament and only scored one goal.

'I'm thirty-one now,' he told Nani. 'Hopefully, I'll play at the 2018 World Cup and maybe Euro 2020 too, but I won't get a better chance than this!'

Portugal were not one of the favourites for the tournament, but it was nice not to feel the pressure for once. They had experienced defenders like Pepe and Ricardo Carvalho in the team, but other than Cristiano and Nani, who would score goals or create chances?

Cristiano knew that it would be tough against the top teams like France, Germany and Spain, but his self-belief was as strong as ever. As captain, it was his responsibility to lead his country to victory.

Portugal got off to a terrible start. With two draws against Iceland and Austria, they were heading out of the tournament in the group stage. Cristiano had missed a penalty against Austria but he refused to give up on his dream.

'Look, we just need to calm down,' he told his teammates. 'Whenever we get the ball, we're rushing it forward to try to score. Let's be more patient and pass it.'

Pepe was impressed by Cristiano's new maturity. He had come a long way from the player who used to throw tantrums on the pitch.

Hungary went 2–1 up but the Portuguese players remembered their captain's message. Nani passed to João Mário on the right wing. His cross was just behind Cristiano. Nevertheless, Cristiano flicked it with his right foot into the far corner of the net.

*Goooooooooooooooooooooooooooooaaaaaaaa
aaaaaaaaaaaaaaaaallllllllllllllllllllllllllllllllllllllllll
ll!!!!!!!!!!!!!!!!!!!!*

'Wow, you made that look so easy!' Nani shouted
as he climbed up on Cristiano's back.

'Come on, I'm not ready to go home yet!'
Cristiano replied.

When Hungary scored again, he couldn't believe
it. What were the defenders doing? Cristiano
screamed at his teammates again and again. It wasn't
good enough.

Ricardo Quaresma, his old rival at Sporting Lisbon,
crossed the ball into the box from the left. Cristiano
timed his clever run to perfection and headed the
ball past the goalkeeper.

*Gooooooooooooooooooooooooooooaaaaaaaaaaaaa
aaaaaaaaaaaaaaalllllllllllllllllllllllllllllllllllll!!!!!!!!!!!!*

'This time, we can't let in another goal!' he
shouted to his players.

The game finished 3–3 and it was enough to put
Portugal into the second round.

'What a crazy match!' Cristiano said to Nani as

they left the field. They both felt very relieved. 'We'll need to play a lot better than that next time.'

Against Croatia, their game plan became clear – Pepe, José Fonte and William Carvalho defended well, and Nani, Cristiano and new teenage sensation Renato Sanches played on the counter-attack. The only problem was scoring goals. After ninety minutes, it was still 0–0.

'Keep going!' Cristiano urged his teammates as they took a short break. 'The goal will come!'

In extra time, Renato ran forward with Nani on his left and Cristiano on his right. He passed to Nani, who crossed to Cristiano. His shot was saved but Ricardo was there to score the winner. Against the odds, Portugal were through to the quarter-finals.

Against Poland, the match went all the way to penalties. Cristiano went first. He didn't want to make his Euro 2012 mistake again. He sent the goalkeeper the wrong way: 1–0!

'Come on!' he roared, turning back to the other players on the halfway line. Their team spirit was very strong.

Portugal scored all five to set up a semi-final against Wales. Cristiano was going head to head with a familiar face.

'They're calling it the "Ronaldo vs Bale" match!' Nani told him.

Cristiano smiled. The media were always comparing him to a rival, but football was eleven versus eleven. After so many years in the public eye, he was used to the attention. Cristiano was fully focused on helping his team to win.

At a corner, he was marked by Wales's smallest defender, James Chester. If the cross was good, Cristiano knew he could outjump him. The cross was perfect and his header was perfect too.

Goooooooooooooooooooooooooooooaaaaaaaaaaaaaa aaaaaaaaaaaaalllllllllllllllllllllllllllllllllllll!!!!!!!!!!!!!!!

He slid along the grass and his teammates joined him. Three minutes later, Nani made it 2–0 and Portugal were heading to another European Championships final.

'Congratulations, you've played so well in this tournament,' Cristiano said to Gareth as they hugged at the final whistle. 'You don't deserve to be on the losing side.'

'Thanks,' his Real Madrid teammate replied. 'Good luck in the final!'

But Cristiano's big day only lasted twenty minutes because of an injury to his left knee. He tried to carry on but he couldn't. As he limped off the pitch, he shook his head in disbelief.

Without their leader, Portugal fought hard and in extra time substitute Éder scored the winner. Cristiano was there on the touchline, cheering on his teammates and giving them advice. The players were doing him proud.

'Keep going!' he shouted. He was so nervous that he could barely watch.

At the final whistle, Cristiano was in tears again. They were the Champions of Europe! As he lifted the trophy high into the sky, he achieved yet another dream.

He had worked so hard to make every dream come true: leaving Madeira to sign for Sporting Lisbon at the age of thirteen; joining Manchester

United at the age of eighteen; becoming Real Madrid's top *galáctico*; winning league titles, Ballon d'Or wins and Champions League trophies; and now, winning Euro 2016 with Portugal.

From street matches in Madeira, Cristiano had risen to become a global icon. 'CR7' was a now a famous brand and he had millions of followers on Twitter and Instagram. He had his own museum and his city, Funchal, had even renamed Madeira's airport 'The Cristiano Ronaldo Airport'.

The special talent had always been there, but Cristiano never stopped learning and improving. From a skilful, selfish teenager, he had turned himself into a mature, professional goalscorer, a superstar and the best player in the world. Every day, Cristiano battled to be the best. And his incredible football adventure was far from over.

Turn the page for a sneak preview of
another brilliant football story by
Matt and Tom Oldfield. . .

GARETH BALE

Available now!

CHAPTER 1

THE NEW *GALÁCTICO*

2 September, 2013

'*El nuevo jugador de Real Madrid, Gareth Bale*'

'Real Madrid's new player, Gareth Bale'.

When they called out his name, the stadium went wild. Thousands of fans clapped and cheered their new record signing. '*Bale! Bale! Bale!*' They chanted his name, the name that many of them already had on their shirts. Gareth couldn't believe it – this wasn't even his debut. He wasn't out there flying down the wing; he was wearing a suit. He could only guess how amazing the atmosphere would be for a game. As he got to his feet and walked up to the stage, he took a long, deep breath and told himself to stay calm. He was no longer the shy boy he once was, but he wasn't yet used to this kind of attention.

But even the butterflies in his stomach couldn't stop the big smile on Gareth's face. This was it; the biggest club in the world and the home of the *Galácticos*, the biggest superstars in the world. Luis Figo, Ronaldo, Raul, David Beckham, Cristiano Ronaldo … and now Gareth Bale. As a child, he'd sat with his father in the stands at local Ninian Park watching his Uncle Chris play, pretending that it was the Bernabéu stadium and that the Cardiff City team was the mighty Real Madrid. Now he was living out that fantasy and this time it was Gareth, not his uncle, who was the star.

As he approached the microphone, Gareth waved to the fans and then to his loved ones. It meant the world to him that they were all here for his big day: his mother Debbie and his father Frank, Grandad Dennis, his older sister Vicky, his best friend Ellis and, of course, his girlfriend Emma and their beautiful young daughter Alba. Without their endless support, he knew he would never have made it here.

When things settled down a bit, Gareth began: *'Es un sueño para mi jugar para Real Madrid. Gracias por esta gran acogida. ¡Hala Madrid!'* These were the first Spanish words he'd learnt and, of course, the most important. He'd practised them for days so that even in the excitement, he wouldn't forget them: 'It's my dream to play for Real Madrid. Thank you for this big welcome. Come on Madrid!' The noise was incredible, so loud that he'd had to pause halfway through.

And then came the moment everyone had been waiting for, especially Gareth. He'd imagined it so many times but this time it was real. The President of Real Madrid held up the famous white shirt and there was his name in big black letters across the back: 'BALE'. The cameras flashed and the crowd roared once more. He was a *Galáctico* now – the most expensive of them all - and so his old Number 3 was no longer good enough. As he had in his last season at Tottenham, now he wore the number of his childhood hero, the Manchester United wing wizard Ryan Giggs – Number 11.

Michael Owen had worn the number at Real Madrid in 2004, as had Arjen Robben in 2007. Gareth was proud to follow in their footsteps but he was determined to make that shirt his own. Watching the scenes around him, he couldn't wait for the biggest challenge of his life. He was the most expensive player in the world and there would be a lot of pressure on him to join his teammate Cristiano Ronaldo as one of the very best players of all time.

As he did keepie-uppies on the Bernabéu pitch, Gareth thought back to his childhood days at Caedelyn Park. As a lightning-fast teenager in Wales, his family and coaches had predicted big things for him but no one had predicted this. At both Southampton and Tottenham, there had been difficult times when injuries looked like they might end Gareth's childhood dream. But the Welsh dragon had battled on and made it to the top.

CRISTIANO RONALDO HONOURS

Manchester United

🏆 Premier League: 2006–07, 2007–08, 2008–09

🏆 FA Cup: 2003–04

🏆 Football League Cup: 2005–06, 2008–09

🏆 Champions League: 2008-09

Real Madrid

🏆 La Liga: 2011–12

🏆 Copa del Rey: 2010–11, 2013–14

🏆 UEFA Champions League: 2013–14, 2015–16

Portugal

🏆 FIFA Under-20 World Cup Golden Ball: 2005

Individual

🏆 UEFA Team of the Year: 2004, 2007, 2008, 2009, 2010, 2011, 2012, 2013, 2014, 2015

🏆 PFA Premier League Team of the Year: 2005–06, 2006–07, 2007–08, 2008–09

🏆 PFA Young Player of the Year: 2006–07

🏆 PFA Players' Player of the Year: 2006–07, 2007–08

🏆 FWA Footballer of the Year: 2006–07, 2007–08

🏆 FIFA FIFPro World XI: 2007, 2008, 2009, 2010, 2011, 2012, 2013, 2014, 2015

🏆 Premier League Golden Boot: 2007–08

🏆 European Golden Shoe: 2007–08, 2010–11, 2013–14, 2014–15

🏆 UEFA Champions League top scorer: 2007–08, 2012–13, 2013–14, 2014–15, 2015–16

🏆 Ballon d'Or: 2008, 2013, 2014, 2016

🏆 FIFA World Player of the Year: 2008

🏆 La Liga top scorer: 2010–11, 2013–14, 2014–15

🏆 La Liga Team of the Season: 2013–14, 2014–15, 2015–16

🏆 La Liga Best Player: 2013–14

🏆 UEFA Best Player in Europe Award: 2014, 2016

RONALDO

(7) THE FACTS

NAME:
Cristiano Ronaldo

DATE OF BIRTH:
5 February 1985

AGE: 32

PLACE OF BIRTH:
Funchal, Madeira

NATIONALITY: Portugal

BEST FRIEND: Nani

CURRENT CLUB: Real Madrid

POSITION: LW

THE STATS

Height (cm):	185
Club appearances:	715
Club goals:	522
Club trophies:	18
International appearances:	138
International goals:	71
International trophies:	1
Ballon d'Ors:	4

★ ★ ★ **HERO RATING: 94** ★ ★ ★

GREATEST MOMENTS

Type and search the web links to see the magic for yourself!

⭐ 1   6TH AUGUST 2003, SPORTING LISBON 3-1 MANCHESTER UNITED

https://www.youtube.com watch?v=QCeGoaaTNsg

This was the moment when Cristiano became a future star. Right-back John O'Shea will never forget this friendly match where a skinny young Sporting winger made a complete fool of him with his speed and skill. Cristiano was the star of the show and by the end of the game, he was a Manchester United player.

2. 21ST MAY 2008, MANCHESTER UNITED 1-1 CHELSEA (6-5 ON PENALTIES)

https://www.youtube.com/watch?v=71CEkjrN8Ko

Cristiano had already won the Premier League title but he was desperate to win the Champions League too. He scored an amazing header to give Manchester United the lead in the final against Chelsea. Cristiano missed a penalty in the shoot-out but his team still went on to win the Double.

3. 16TH APRIL 2009, PORTO 0-1 MANCHESTER UNITED

https://www.youtube.com/watch?v=NksLn_VUjll

Cristiano has scored loads of amazing goals but they don't get any better than this strike in the Champions League semi-final. From forty yards out, the ball flew like an arrow into the top corner. Thanks to Cristiano's wondergoal, Manchester United were through to another Champions League final.

4   24TH MAY 2014, REAL MADRID 4-1 ATLÉTICO MADRID

https://www.youtube.com/watch?v=Ji021RYgGXQ

The Real Madrid fans had been waiting 11 years for 'La Décima', their tenth Champions League trophy. Cristiano's goals got them all the way to the 2014 final and his penalty in extra-time gave them the victory. He took off his shirt and roared like the Incredible Hulk.

5   10TH JULY 2016, PORTUGAL 1-0 FRANCE

https://www.youtube.com/watch?v=Qd82YFfAXYI

After leading his country to the Euro 2016 final, Cristiano got injured early on against France. He was devastated to miss the biggest game of his life but from the bench, he cheered and coached his team to victory. At the final whistle, Cristiano was there to lift the trophy.

PLAY LIKE YOUR HEROES

THE CRISTIANO RONALDO GOAL CELEBRATION

SEE IT HERE You**Tube**

https://www.youtube.com/watch?v=EjuOjDvpscs&t=14s

STEP 1: Score an amazing goal.

STEP 2: Run towards the fans, smiling, nodding and pointing at yourself.

STEP 3: As you get towards the corner flag, jump into the air with your arms up high.

STEP 4: In mid-air, spin around so that you now have your back to the fans and they can all see the name and number on the back of your shirt.

STEP 5: As you land, keep your feet wide apart and bring your arms down dramatically until they are slightly behind your body.

STEP 6: Scream loudly with your mouth wide open in an 'O' shape.

STEP 7: Hold that pose until all of your team-mates run over and hug you.

TEST YOUR KNOWLEDGE

QUESTIONS

1. Why did Dolores and Dinis choose the name 'Ronaldo' for their fourth child?

2. How old was Cristiano when he left Madeira and where did he go?

3. Who was Cristiano's biggest rival in the Sporting youth team?

4. How old was Cristiano when he made his first-team debut for Sporting Lisbon, and what shirt number did he wear?

5. Who was Sir Alex Ferguson looking to replace at Manchester United when he signed Cristiano?

6. Which Manchester United teammate did Cristiano clash with at the 2006 World Cup, and why?

7. Who was the Manchester United first-team coach who helped to make Cristiano an even better goalscorer?

8. How much did Real Madrid pay to sign Cristiano in 2009?

9. What shirt number did Cristiano wear when he first arrived at Real Madrid and why?

10. How many Champions League finals has Cristiano played in and how many goals has he scored?

11. How many major international tournaments has Cristiano played in for Portugal?

Answers below. . . No cheating!

1. Dolores liked the actor and President of the United States, Ronald Reagan. **2.** He was 12 years old and he went to Lisbon. **3.** Ricardo Quaresma **4.** He was 17 years old and he wore Number 28. **5.** David Beckham. **6.** Wayne Rooney. Cristiano helped to get him sent off when England played Portugal in the quarter-finals. **7.** René Meulensteen. **8.** £80million. **9.** He wore Number 9 because club legend Raúl already wore Number 7. **10.** He has played in five finals (2008, 2009, 2014, 2016, 2017) and he has scored four goals, plus a penalty in the 2016 shoot-out. **11.** Seven (Euro 2004, World Cup 2006, Euro 2008, Euro 2008, World Cup 2010, Euro 2012, Euro 2014, World Cup 2014, Euro 2016).

HAVE YOU GOT THEM ALL?

ULTIMATE FOOTBALL HEROES

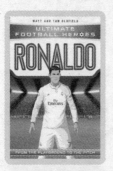